TERENCE TRENT D'ARBY

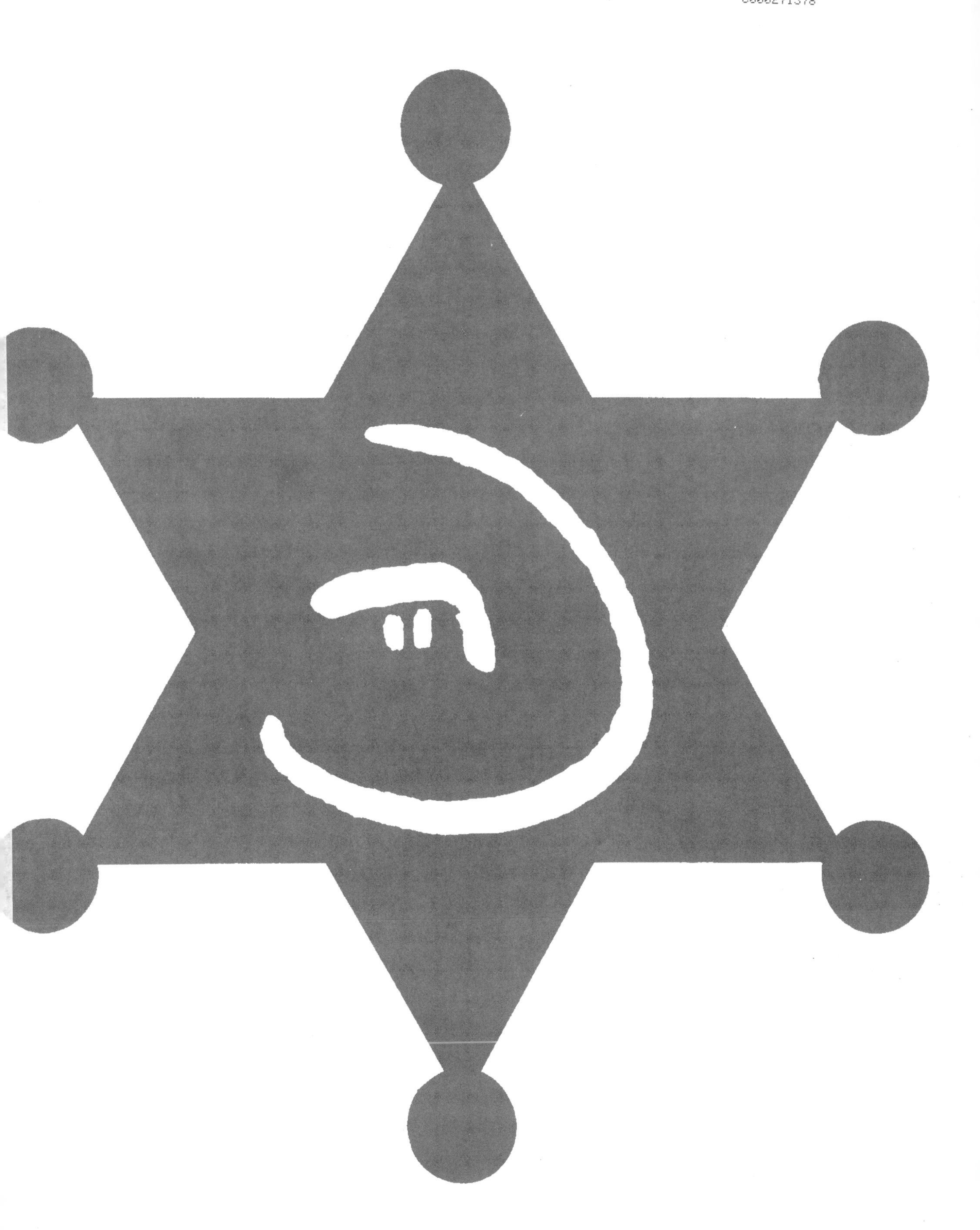

TERENCE TRENT D'ARBY

DAISANN McLANE

BLOOMSBURY

First published in Great Britain 1989
Bloomsbury Publishing Limited, 2 Soho Square, London W1V 5DE

A CIP catalogue record for this book
is available from the British Library

ISBN 0-7475-0321-4

PICTURE CREDITS
All Action Photographic 17, 26, 29, 33, 37, 45, 50, 64, 67, 77, 93, 99;
London Features *back cover*, 10, 27, 48, 52, 53, 54, 57, 68, 74, 89,
100–101, 103; Valerie Hood 76; Pictorial Press 24, 30, 55, 110, 112, 117;
Barry Plummer 51, 95; Retna 8–9, 12–13, 18, 38, 71, 81, 114, 102;
Rex Features *front cover*, 14, 16, 20, 34, 42, 44, 46, 49, 60–61, 78, 84–85,
92, 94, 102, 104, 108–109, 115; Richard Young 113

Designed by Fielding Rowinski
Typeset by Bookworm Typesetting, Manchester
Printed by Butler & Tanner Limited, Frome and London

ACKNOWLEDGEMENTS

There are many people who gave me invaluable advice, information and assistance on this project. For getting the whole ball rolling, I have to thank Kit Rachlis, my editor at the **Village Voice**, who gave me the original D'Arby assignment, supported and advised me through every step of the long, exciting investigative process, then did a terrific job of helping me get my thoughts in order, and into print. Thanks, too, go to my **Voice** colleagues R J Smith, Bill Bastone and Chuck Eddy, for helping me through the labyrinths of US Army bureaucracy. Also in New York, I was able to pick up the trail of D'Arby's German years thanks to the assistance of Roger Trilling, Mike Knuth, Andrien Kreye and Kurt Loder. The New York critics' mafia, particularly Jon Pareles, Greg Tate and John Swenson, also gave me some much-needed perspectives, and a helping hand. I am especially grateful to Nelson George for sharing with me his astute, considered analysis of D'Arby.

I went to DeLand, Florida as a stranger; I was received with unexpected warmth, hospitality, and friendship wherever I went. The principal's staff at Deland High School patiently answered my questions, and dug out their old yearbooks for me. The staff of the **DeLand Sun News** was very open and helpful, especially Nancy Stinson. Special thanks go to Valerie Hood, who was incredible – she even managed to take photographs of DeLand and the high school for this book in the week before she was moving to England!

This book would simply have been impossible without the help, unselfish assistance, advice and guidance of Karen Kirkpatrick. She guided me through DeLand, gave me access to her D'Arby files, and to her own, excellently reported and written pieces. And, for many months afterwards, she continued to guide me in my understanding of D'Arby. I can't thank her enough for her help, or for her friendship.

I'm also grateful to the Reverend James Benjamin and Frances Darby and their family for opening their doors to me, and allowing me to see the side of their son that he didn't. My interview with them was a turning point in my understanding of D'Arby. As was my talk with Stan Whitted, who graciously answered my many questions, and provided keen and thoughtful insights into D'Arby's development as a student and a singer.

This book would also have been, quite literally, impossible without the technical assistance of Robert Davidson, who got my computer up and running, and held my hand through the process. Likewise Mike Mazzella of Information Products, who took care of me when the damn thing blew up in the middle of the book.

On the UK side of things, many thanks to Gloria Ferris and Rivers Scott for finding a home for this project, and providing long-distance support and encouragement. Also to David Reynolds, for his patient, sympathetic editing. Thanks to **NME**'s Paolo Hewitt and Denis Campbell, and also to Vivien Goldman, for giving me their thoughts on the D'Arby phenomenon. And to Mark Soich, Patricia Gillan and John Armstrong, for friendship and advice.

I'm grateful to my friends for their advice and comments and encouragement, in particular my **Voice** colleagues Jan Hoffman and Enrique Fernandez. Galen Brandt, my best friend, patiently listened as I read my preliminary drafts, and her ideas and counsel were invaluable. Finally, this book would have been impossible to finish without the love and support of my parents, Edward and Olivia McLane, and it is to them that I dedicate this effort.

Brooklyn, NY 1989

CONTENTS

TheRetur

N

1

nof the ative

chapter

The Return of the Native

It was a fabulous assignment for any journalist – the chance to do the very first American interview with an up-and-coming new international rock star. Already the subject of dozens of profiles in overseas magazines, he is established as controversial, outspoken, with the added fascination of having a mysterious past.

A thick file of press material arrives from the record company: he appears to be articulate, talkative and eminently quotable: a perfect subject.

The interview does not start well.

The new international rock star lies stretched out on a black leather couch. His eyes are bloodshot, and he's half asleep: he doesn't seem to want to talk to anybody, especially a journalist.

'Ehhhhhh . . . this conversation is like, uh, bending my sense of consciousness at the moment. You know those times where you think you're going crazy? Those times are becoming more and more frequent for me . . .'

'But really, I don't wanna talk about this. . . . Let's talk about music. Just music . . .'

(Sighs) 'At the moment I just . . . you're pulling me back to a place where I really don't want to go at the moment. Right now, you're

reopening a past that I don't particularly want to go to. For whatever reason, God only knows. . . .'

'I'm really tired. I'm sorry about that. I'm not as coherent as I usually am. Uhhh . . . would you like some tea?'

Panic sets in. The editor's never going to believe that you sat for almost two hours with the man famous for his amazingly quotable **bon mots** without getting a great story.

But then you calm down. You begin to notice many things about the fellow that you wouldn't if he was charming you with cleverness, or engaging you in razor-sharp repartee. For example, his accent, which changes, in the space of a sentence, from a London wide-boy's to a Southern American drawl. Then there's his manner, which alternates between endearing and surly, self-confident and insecure.

He is obviously a man of a thousand faces, a natural actor creating new roles as you watch. But which one is real? And how did he come to be lounging in this high-level office, with a promising album and millions of dollars of record-company promotion money behind him?

It's not what he says, but what he leaves out that is fascinating.

And, after several weeks spent phoning, researching, inquiring and investigating, at last the beginning of the trail is uncovered: a kind and gentle American town, where everybody remembers Terence Trent – 'Terry' – Darby.

Terence Trent D'Arby had a few good reasons to be out-of-sorts during the interview on that chilly January afternoon in 1988. The most immediate was a bad hangover. The night before, he had attended the Rock and Roll Hall of Fame awards dinner in New York, a celebrity-studded music industry bash, and he'd ended up partying all night downtown. Hence, the bloodshot eyes. But there were other, more fundamental reasons for his uneasiness.

This was D'Arby's second official visit to the US since his massive success in the UK (his first trip over, in November 1987, had been a quick one-week showcase tour of New York, Los Angeles and several other big American cities). This time his album, **The Hardline According to Terence Trent D'Arby**, was in the stores, and his American record company, CBS, was promoting it heavily. In fact, they were pushing D'Arby as if he were an already-established mega-star, not a 26-year-old novice. During this short visit, D'Arby was scheduled to appear on the big three television programmes, the Today Show, Entertainment Tonight and MTV – an unheard of coup for a singer who didn't yet have a hit in America.

The music-biz hotline buzzed with talk that D'Arby was number one priority on the CBS records list. According to the rumours, CBS was going to spare no effort – or expense – to make this newcomer a star. It was a strategy that made perfect sense. Already, Terence Trent D'Arby had the UK fans and press neatly tucked into his tight black denim jeans-pocket. Why shouldn't he be able to win over in the American market, too? In London, D'Arby had proved his skill not only as a musician, but in the more difficult – and crucial – business of image-making.

Even before any of his music reached the public, D'Arby was a certified Media Event. In 1986, the **New Musical Express** put the boyish, unknown singer on their cover, with the headline: NEW PRINCE OF POP. Many more magazine covers and major features followed that first one. In a few months, those mile-wide cheekbones and braided dreadlocks were as well-known in British households as Princess Di's hairstyles and the Queen Mother's hats. D'Arby was everywhere. Of course the music papers couldn't get enough of him, but he also captivated the fashion world, the trendies, the tabloids, and more: **The Face**, the **News Of The World**, even the **Sunday Times**! He was model-handsome, and he said outrageous things that made superb headlines. 'I like making love,' he told **Record Mirror**. 'I make love as often as I wash my hair.' To Denis Campbell of **NME** he stated, 'I think I'm a genius. Point fucking blank.' When his **Hardline** LP finally hit the stores in July 1987, it sold a million copies in three days. By the end of the year, D'Arby could boast a double platinum LP that had collected favourable reviews from virtually every UK critic.

'Designer soul' was the label the British press coined to describe D'Arby's music, which really wasn't one style, but a whole fashion catalogue. The songs on **Hardline** highlighted D'Arby's skill of slipping in and out of different modes of classic r&b and soul. On his Top-Ten UK singles, 'If You Let Me Stay', and 'Wishing Well', he demonstrated an uncanny gift for mimicry, and his singing echoed a half-dozen or more of the great legends of soul music. The critics had an endless list of comparisons: Sam Cooke, Stevie Wonder, Michael Jackson, Prince, Marvin Gaye, as well as Little Richard, Tina Turner, and Mick Jagger.

CBS's US publicity campaign carried the D'Arby hoopla even further, and made the British critical response seem positively lukewarm by comparison. 'The Hardline slowly evolved,' reads his original CBS biographical press release (an extraordinary three-page, single-spaced document that D'Arby later had rewritten, because he thought it was too revealing). '... Here is where the Rolling Stones rub shoulders with Bogart, where T. Rex and Sly Stone dance alongside James Brown and Muhammad Ali, where the rebelliousness of Jerry Lee Lewis and Marvin Gaye, and the spine-chilling voices of Aretha and Patsy Cline all take "exile on Main Street" ...'

The D'Arby press pack is remarkable not only for its length (most new acts get one page, and that's it), but for its tone; it does not attempt to convince its readers that Terence Trent D'Arby is the next Dylan/Springsteen/Second Coming. It assumes he already is. Even veteran rock writers who think they've read it all gasped at the lead paragraph: 'A rebel by nature, stubborn and uncompromising in his art and lifestyle, accused of arrogance by default, a self-described "lovable rogue" who's the first to admit, "You may not like me at first, but there'll come a time when you need somebody to talk to you can trust, and you'll say to yourself, 'well, that bastard did tell me the truth'!" This is it: THE HARDLINE ACCORDING TO TERENCE TRENT D'ARBY.'

That was only the half of it. The Terence Trent D'Arby American package also included a custom-printed colour folder, and a silver-toned sheriff's badge inlaid with the D'Arby logo (the initials 'TTD' in the shape of a face) that also appears in the middle of the customized red CBS label of his album. Subtle signals that all indicate one thing: money is being spent. This D'Arby fellow is a big deal.

With all the excitement and support surrounding his US promo visit, you'd expect D'Arby to be confident, cool, and to sit back and enjoy the ride. But the situation – like D'Arby – was more complex than that. This may have been the inauguration of his career in the United States, but D'Arby was on very familiar territory; he is in fact American. A US citizen, he was

born and raised in the States, and had even served in Uncle Sam's Army. Luck of the draw and a series of serendipitous circumstances had made him the

toast of Europe and the UK, not of his native country. And now he was back to see what could happen over here . . . but suppose nothing did? It's one thing to be the r&b king of Great Britain, but over here, D'Arby would be facing serious home-grown competition. Much of his moodiness during his first interview in New York can be attributed to simple jitters; he must have been apprehensive about coming home.

And home – the US – is one place where Terence Trent D'Arby

didn't particularly want to be. At least that's what he'd been telling the British press, over and over again. 'To my mind, America is the most racist, sexist, homophobic, violent society in the so-called free world,' he announced to an **NME** reporter only six months before his US debut. In England, he had fashioned himself as the angry exile, and his role as *enfant terrible* (not to mention his anti-Americanism) endeared him to press and fans alike.

D'Arby had been especially outspoken on the subject of racism, and he complained articulately and at length to interviewers about the games that American black artists were forced to play in order to have a successful 'crossover' musical career in the United States. Games that he refused to play, and if that meant he couldn't be as huge a success in America as he was in England, too bad. 'I don't care about the States if it means I have to compromise, but I *do* care if it means I can go through and just shake fucking shit up,' he told Charles Shaar Murray of **Q** in September, 1987. He went on to reiterate what he'd already said to a half-dozen other British journalists – that he would not 'have his balls cut off' for pop stardom like so many other black American artists. 'Prince has had to play the bisexual image, Jackson's had to be asexual ... it's like, in the contract, it certifies them to a free plastic surgeon visitation, guarantees them a make-up artist at all times to lighten 'em up for photographs if you sell more than two million albums, and these guys wouldn't do or say anything that would make them lose more than one record sale ...' When Murray responded to this by observing, quite astutely, that rap acts like Run DMC had managed to sell millions of records without compromising themselves as black men, or by getting nose jobs, D'Arby waxed testy. Run DMC, he contended, was an urban black act, not a mainstream pop band, and that was different. 'I'm trying to prove that you can be a massive crossover success without chopping off your dick!'

D'Arby talked tough; in the UK, his was indeed a 'hardline'. But now he was back in the USA, where he'd have to come up with more than words. The one-time Golden Gloves champ had boxed himself right into a corner: if he *didn't* try to challenge the US music industry and its racial stereotypes, he risked looking like a fool – or worse – in London, where he was pretty close to being a hero. However, if he decided to give the American reporters and television interviewers his complete, uncensored view on racism, the US and the music business, he might be ruining the biggest opportunity of his career. Because he was right; how many black faces ever make it to the cover of mainstream music-biz magazines like **Rolling Stone**? Michael Jackson's clip, 'Beat It', was a classic that set the style for hundreds of rock videos to imitate – but it only got onto MTV's programming rotation after aggressive lobbying by Jackson's record company. If Terence Trent D'Arby stuck to his hardline, there was every possibility that he'd be shut out of the US pop arena altogether.

'Black Rock' is the not-so-affectionate nickname of the building that houses the offices of CBS/Sony Records on 52nd Street in Manhattan, New York. In its drawing-board stage, the CBS skyscraper must have seemed like a brilliant concept; a visionary, contemporary 36-storey column of ebony stone created by the late Finnish architect Eero Saarinen, renowned the world over for his design of the United Nations building. What better image could there be for a company that was, at once, conservative and maverick? CBS was a corporation secure in its position as the number one broadcast network in America, but whose highest profits now came from a venture as fickle as the weather, as reliable as a schoolgirl's crush – the business of popular music.

Since the late fifties, CBS Records has built its reputation on its ability to discover and develop major new pop acts – thanks largely to the talent-scouting prowess of the division's first president, John Hammond Senior.

It was Hammond who, back in the fifties and sixties, acquired Bob Dylan and Miles Davis for the CBS label; his last signing before he retired was a promising young singer-songwriter from New Jersey named Bruce Springsteen. Hammond's strategy – to find a few potentially major acts, and then spend lots of time and money breaking them into the marketplace – continues to influence the philosophy and direction of the company. More than any other US label, CBS is stable for superstars in the business of grooming and coddling platinum-calibre artists.

They've had their share of flops. Most notable was their failure to make Elvis Costello a superstar in the early eighties. When Costello landed in America he received the full CBS 'treatment' – trendy press parties, a clever advertising campaign, a 'no interviews' policy, supported by relentless stream of hype from the publicity staff. But it didn't work. Elvis failed to conquer America in the mega-buck, hit-single way that CBS had anticipated, despite the enthusiastic support of the rock press.

D'Arby's marketing strategy echoed the Costello campaign. So did the initial press hype. There would be a few, limited, and highly-selective interviews, mostly for television. The interview that I was granted, as a reporter for the **Village Voice**, took place only after several weeks of back-and-forth negotiation between the editor, Kit Rachlis, and the CBS vice-president of publicity, Marilyn Laverty.

The game played by a magazine and a record company publicity department is standard operating procedure in US rock journalism. The publicist, obviously, wants front-page exposure for the artist, in the most prestigious publications, with the assurance that the resulting piece will be completely favourable. The magazine editor wants unlimited access to the artist (as opposed to a controlled, half-hour interview monitored by the publicist), an 'exclusive' (not an artist who's going to be on the cover of 15 other magazines the same week), and a critical, hard-hitting story, one that will sell well at the newsstands. Usually this game is brief – editors and publicists alike know it well, and they quickly get down to business. But in D'Arby's case it was more elaborate.

First came the warm-ups. D'Arby was extremely special, Marilyn Laverty insisted: 'History will prove that Terence Trent D'Arby is a major artist.' She made frequent references to Elvis Costello, Springsteen, Dylan. The upshot? Terence Trent D'Arby should be guaranteed the cover of the **Voice** if he agreed to an interview.

No way, responded Kit Rachlis. The **Voice** doesn't work that way. It's not professional journalism. Besides, if we were going to do a major feature, we'd need an extra-long interview, say two hours, plus additional informal time with D'Arby later.

After a week or two Laverty

conceded that it was all right if there was no guaranteed cover, as long as the piece was a 'major' feature. D'Arby, according to Laverty, really wanted to talk to the **Voice**. There were no plans to talk to any other print media, she said, not even **Rolling Stone**. Just one thing – D'Arby wanted to know who would be his interviewer. Could Rachlis put together a dossier of material from the journalist who would be writing the piece?

TTD

I complied, thinking that this was a rather unusual preliminary. Neither I nor my colleagues had ever before been asked for *our* résumé prior to an interview; with one rather notorious exception, in the case of Yoko Ono. A friend of mine once interviewed John Lennon, but had to submit his date, place and time of birth beforehand to Yoko Ono so she could calculate his astrological chart and examine it carefully for potential bad vibes before she gave her approval to the meeting.

Actually, the fact that D'Arby wanted to take the trouble to read some of my work implied that he took the business of interviewing more seriously than most rock stars. I'd found out, through the grapevine, that he was a knowledgeable and assiduous reader of the music press. Peter Guralnick, author of several distinguished books on blues and r&b, had met D'Arby backstage after his Boston showcase concert. Much to Guralnick's surprise, D'Arby had approached him like a fan, then asked him informed questions about his last book.

D'Arby was scheduled to come to New York for the last week of January. Rachlis and Laverty finally came to a general agreement: there would be a 'major' feature, but only if D'Arby was forthcoming during the two-hour interview. He would be unaccompanied by publicists. Afterwards, there would be an opportunity to spend time with him more informally although the details were unspecified. It was understood that this would be D'Arby's only major press interview during this time.

And so, I began the daunting task of sifting through the pages and pages of previously published features and interviews, in which D'Arby revealed his position on everything from safe sex (he doesn't bother) to Margaret Thatcher (guess). He seemed to have an opinion about everything under the sun, and it seemed as though his every utterance had been dutifully recorded by the British press.

However, it became clear that there were things that Terence Trent D'Arby had left unsaid. He had lots of opinions about music, politics, people, and what he was trying to do in his career. But when

the subject rolled around to himself, his family background, and his years in America, he became much less articulate, and often betrayed feelings of sadness, and bitterness. The glimpses he did reveal were fascinating: he was a preacher's son, an ex-Golden Gloves boxer (the Golden Gloves is the major US organization for amateur pugilists), an ex-journalist, and a court-martialled soldier who barely escaped imprisonment for running away from the Army in Germany. Was any, part, or all of the D'Arby legend true?

As I played the **Hardline** album, I became more curious about the personality behind the image. D'Arby's music seemed so out-of-touch with what was happening in the current American black music scene. On **Hardline**, he'd created a high-tech time capsule of the hip sounds of 20 years ago. Moreover, he seemed to be doing this

artlessly, without the sense of history or irony that someone like Prince projects when he quotes or revives retro black pop styles. I wondered if D'Arby lacked this sense of historical reference to black pop because he didn't grow up listening to it. (If he'd had a truly Christian upbringing, 'worldly' music wouldn't have been heard in the home.) His American background, and particularly his experiences in the fundamentalist Christian church, seemed to be the key to his music. Is that where he'd discovered his talent for singing? (The Terence Trent D'Arby who composed and sang the haunting, gospel-toned 'As Yet Untitled' was surely no stranger to the House of the Lord.) Where had he actually lived with his family? – in some of the British articles he'd mentioned New York, in others Chicago, but my guess was that he wasn't raised in an urban setting. Was his family poor, middle-class, well-to-do? Had he been in trouble as an adolescent? (His interviews implied that he'd been an alienated 'bad boy'.) And what had happened to him in the US that made England seem a safe haven from 'the most racist nation in the world'?

On the afternoon I arrived at Black Rock, signed my name in the security register, and took the sleek, silent elevator up to the Publicity Department office, I had lots and lots of questions for Terence Trent D'Arby.

chapter 2

Bad D

ay at Black Rock?

Bad Day at Black Rock?

'He's very nervous about meeting you. He's also very, very tired,' Marilyn Laverty confided, in a hushed tone. The CBS publicity director invited me to follow her down a long corridor, into an unoccupied cubicle that contained a long table and some padded swivel chairs. The cell-like, no-nonsense rows of offices contrasted sharply with the overflow of music-biz paraphernalia. Everywhere you looked, there were gold or platinum albums, posters and cardboard stand-ups of the company's artists, piles and stacks of records: pop chaos, but under firm control.

'Terence will be out in a minute with Claudine,' Laverty said.

Claudine? But we've agreed that this is supposed to be a one-to-one interview . . .

'Claudine is his publicist, but she does a little of everything, and he really would be so much more comfortable with her sitting in on the interview,' Laverty replied sheepishly.

This was not good news. The 'babysitter' interview, in which a publicist or manager sits in with the star while the journalist is asking questions (in order, one supposes, to prevent star from planting foot in mouth) is one of the most annoying situations in feature journalism. I was able, eventually, to convince Laverty of this. She disappeared for a moment, and returned with Claudine, an elegant blonde in her late thirties with a French accent. Following her, wearing a huge soft black cap, black jersey shirt, black jeans, and ultra-black RayBan sunglasses, was Terence Trent D'Arby.

D'Arby offered his hand, smiled, then paced itchily around the cubicle, casing the joint. 'Uh, can we, like, do this in some other room? This room makes me feel, uh, like I'm having my conjugal visit. Why don't we use *your* office?' he suggested to Laverty.

Claudine vanished. Laverty escorted us into her private office, then she vanished, too. D'Arby sprawled himself across Laverty's black leather couch, and made himself quite at home.

'All right,' he said. 'Let's talk.'

With D'Arby reclining on the couch, and me sitting in a chair alongside, I felt a bit like an analyst waiting for the patient to describe last night's dream. I decided that the best approach was to be totally straightforward. So I began by telling D'Arby that I'd read his biographical material, and that I was interested in doing a different kind of article than the ones that had appeared in England. The style of the **Voice**, I explained, is to write in-depth, substantive profiles, not publicity stuff. D'Arby nodded thoughtfully, and said he understood; he reads the **Village Voice**. I told him I thought the American audience would want to know more about his life in the US, how he grew up, how that influenced his music, and how he got from here all the way to the top of the pops. D'Arby chuckled good-naturedly, and seemed to relax a bit. I pulled out my notes, turned on the tape recorder and began at the beginning:

Do you know anything about your family heritage?
(TTD) I've got lots of stuff in my blood, I can't say exactly where the deep, deep roots are from. There's Irish, there's Spanish, there's two different kinds of Indian. Lots of stuff. I pick up bits of information here and there from my mother and grandmother.
Tell me about your grandmother.
I used to stay with her a lot. My father would be out running revival meetings and I would stay in school so I would be with her a lot. It was my father's mother. She was really straight, but really supportive at the same time. You never doubted for a moment that when she spanked you it was for anything less than what she firmly believed was right at the time.
Is D'Arby your real name?
Yes. When I was a kid I hated my name. I never imagined someday people would be asking me if it was real.
Tell me about your father.
My father was Reverend Darby. Elder Darby. He's a Pentecostal. The Church of Our Lord Jesus Christ. On the evangelist circuit he's very well respected.
So you mostly grew up in New Jersey?
Ahhh . . . (*suddenly begins to sound impatient.*) It was a long time ago. I spent a long time all over the place. Look, I was born in New York, and I lived here until I was two. So I can't really say I grew up here. From two until six I lived in East Orange, New Jersey; from six to nine I lived in Florida, from nine to 11 I lived in Chicago, and from 11 to 18 I lived in Florida. Then I lived in South Carolina first, and then Oklahoma, and then, um, I moved to Munich, lived there for a couple of years and then moved to London. I moved to London permanently two years ago. I knew it very well before I settled there. I was always going over there for different things when I was still in Germany. Projects. And I was going out with someone from there as well, so I would go over there a lot.
Your mother, you've mentioned in some interviews, was a well-known gospel singer?
Yes. She was well-known in the context of the church organization my parents belong to. Her name is Frances Darby. Her father was a pastor, and she was brought up in the tradition.
What was the 'tradition', and what sort of preacher was your dad?
It was definitely a charismatic movement, it relied on speaking in tongues and the casting out of the devil. Baptism is by full immersion in water. I can only say that, in front of his children, my father practised what he preached. Too many preachers don't, and that is why to this day I have a . . . well, I can take a lot of things from people, but I can't take hypocrisy very well. Blatant hypocrisy. We're all humans, we're all hypocrites to some degree, but I can't stand blatant hypocrisy. Simply because I've seen too many people get up in a pulpit and preach about one thing on a Sunday, then turn around and get into bed with someone else's wife. And that has left a very nasty taste in my mouth. To my mind, that exhibits a grand degree of hypocrisy.

You grow up in the church and you see everything, you see life.

The problem with it is that too often the life they convince you they want you to lead – the life they *tell* you to lead – isn't a human life at all. It's a super-human life. We're humans. So many fall by the wayside, just by virtue of being humans. But if you're brought up as a child to believe that this is the way things are supposed to be, and then you see people being condemned for nothing less than being human, and exhibiting the capacity for human error, you get disillusioned. And it takes a long while to get over it. I was reading about this organization that was formed to help people adjust to life who have been brought up in fundamentalist backgrounds. Their lives are a shambles, they're dazed and confused and they're trying to run away from some sense of impending doom and gloom.

What was it like for you, growing up in a Pentecostal environment?

As a child, you believe in it. You also believe in Santa Claus and they take that away from you and eventually, well . . . When you grow up as a kid in that environment and you don't know anything else but the situation you grow up in, that's what's normal for you. After a while, it becomes stifling when you start going out with your peers who are able to do all sorts of things that you aren't allowed to do. You start to measure your life to theirs, and all of a sudden it becomes . . . Your peers start to make fun of you, they piss all over you, and slowly you come to resent the life that you've been led to by your parents. Now they're doing nothing but raising you the way they believe they're obligated to raise you as good Christians.

Were you closer to your mother or your father?

I've always been closer to my mother (*immediately, no hesitation*). That's something you can ask all the people around me. What I mean by that is the closeness to my mother affects all the other relationships in life with the people around me. Yeah, I'm definitely a mama's boy.

Where is she now?

In Florida, uh, Daytona Beach. DeLand.

Where's DeLand?

Outside Daytona Beach in Central Florida. That's where I lived from 11 to 18. The formative years (*laughs ironically*).I went to high school there, DeLand High School.

Is that where they had you in some sort of school for gifted children?

No, that was when I was in Chicago. Apparently I had some kind of high IQ. I was in a class for gifted kids, we had special classes and once a week we went to the University of Chicago. I think, in retrospect, that it was a situation like this: they got some really intelligent black children together, and it was almost like we were being studied ourselves.

So were you a precocious child?

At one point I had this massive vocabularly. The first book I

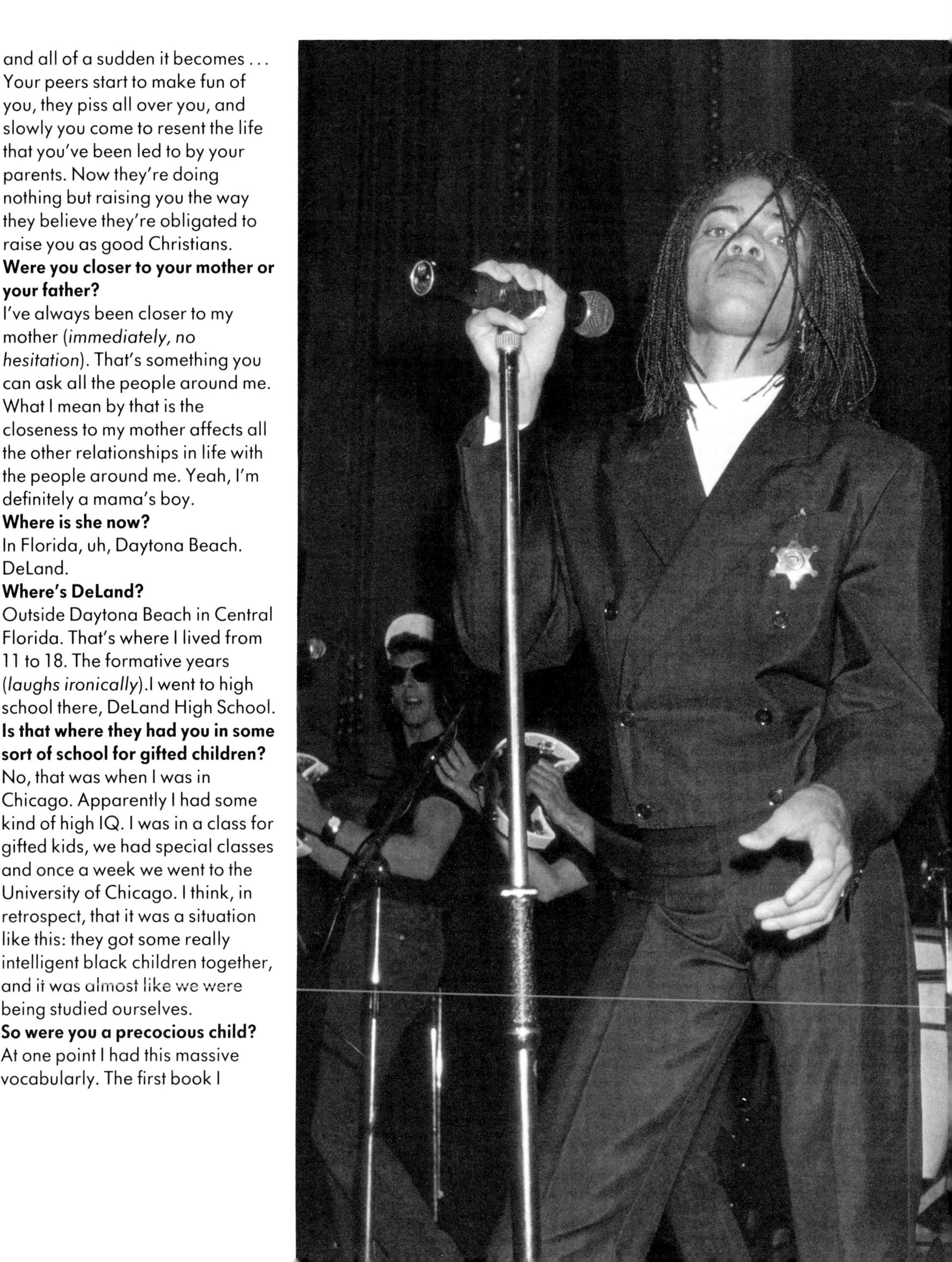

TTD

remember taking an interest in as a child was the dictionary.

Not the Bible?

Hmmmmmph! I've only started to become more interested in the more poetic aspects of the Bible recently, now that it no longer has this mind-altering sway over me. Now I'm really free to look at it for what it is, a piece of literature.

But anyway, back to your special school . . .

Yeah, well we probably were being studied. All of us react to our condition in a racist society in different ways. If you're made to believe you're stupid, you probably will turn out that way.

Me, I was motivated. I read from an early age. I remember my father coming home with this enormous book, this big red Webster's Dictionary. It was fascinating. It had all these words in it, and I could look them up. It was like a big treasure chest to me.

Besides which . . . I used to get into so much trouble as a kid. My generation was the first in the South to be completely integrated. I went to an all black school until I was in the first grade, then we had to mix with the white kids and it was like the world changed so dramatically. I was always in trouble for being a loudmouth, being too smart for my own good, always wanting to be the centre of attention. And the thing I was thinking about the other day, when someone was asking me if success changed me, prompted me to think that the way journalists tend to react now is no different from the way teachers reacted to me then. I've not really changed a bit. I'm still talking too much, have the same desire for attention that I did then, and I'm still misunderstood in similar ways. You've got to understand about the double standard that existed. If Johnny was white, and spoke out first, he was 'outspoken'. If his peers reacted to him, then he was a 'natural born leader'. But with me, the same characteristics meant I was a loudmouth. That I disrupted the class. It was very confusing, and at that time I was, for some reason, much lighter-skinned as well. Black kids didn't accept me, white kids didn't either. It was difficult.

But your parents must have been leaders in the black community, being pastor of a church and all, so weren't you accepted because of that?

Yes, they were accepted. But they weren't part of the black bourgeoisie. And inside of the black world there was this going on, the lighter you were, the more attention you got. Then with other people, the lighter you were, the more venom they showed towards you. It was schizophrenic.

What is your family's class background?

We weren't rich, and we weren't poor. It was probably a lower middle class existence. My father made sure we got all of what we needed and most of what we wanted. We always lived in decent neighbourhoods in good houses. There were times when we had to stay in circumstances that weren't the best. We moved a lot.

Tell me about DeLand.

Oh man! (*sounds extremely irritated*) Uhhh . . . A very sleepy town. It's the sort of town where if you don't have a sense of ambition, you'll be born there, live there, and you'll die there. It's a *very* sleepy town. But dreamers can never be stopped from

dreaming. If they have ambition they're basically on their way. DeLand. DeLand . . . It's very quiet. Typical of America in the 1970s.

We lived in the projects (*note: US version of council houses*) when we first moved there. They were very modern projects in the sense that they were designed very well, you had some land as well as a nice place to live. Then we moved into a house – my parents bought a house and they still live there. They're still together.

I didn't really start appreciating my father until I left home. I've always had a really strong individual streak. Never taken well to authority. And I would rebel. I thought my own character wasn't being given enough space.

Were you the only son?

No, I wasn't the only son, at the time I was living home there were five of us but now there are six. I always wanted an elder sister, I never wanted to be the eldest son. But then, at the same time, the eldest in families tend to be the most successful.

I wasn't a bad child, I just wasn't a conformist. Conformity never really sat well with me. If you have a spirit that's full of wanderlust, you tend to know that as soon as you get your chance that . . . there will be a jailbreak in cell block number nine tonight at 12 o'clock . . . I just knew that DeLand wasn't going to be where I wound up, and I would always say to people, I'm going to do this, and I'm going to do that. I knew that I had to get out, that I could make nothing that I wanted to make in this place.

I read one interview where you said you wanted CBS to make you a star before your tenth high school reunion.

This is true. I mean that. My tenth high school reunion is next year. I graduated in 1979, so next year will be the time I will go back and just rub it in people's faces.

Whose faces?

The people I went to school with and that gave me shit. You know, just people in general. I can't be specific.

(*He sounds extremely irritable. When we started the interview, his accent was quite British. But now it starts to sound American. As he's remembering high school, his speech changes to being mumbly, whiny.*)

It's people, a lot of people. You try to get their attention and they don't want yours. Now, I'm sure, they're ringing up my parents and saying, 'Aw, tell him I called, I was a friend of his.' The typical story. You know, all the people that you told, 'I'm gonna do *this* one day,' and they say, 'Yeah, sure.' Well, now I can go back and show them, I'm doing it. The great thing is, in these situations, you don't have to say anything. You just be very very nice to them. You know they treated you like shit, and they know they treated you like shit. But you never own up to it, and you just make a very quick excuse to leave again. You say to them, 'What are you doing?' and they'll say 'Well, right now I'm sort of working in a 7–11 [*shop*],' and you say to them, with a very concerned look on your face, 'Hey, that's all right, it's a job. We all can't be doing exactly what we want to be doing.' And you say these things very subtly, and you make them feel like shit. Then you leave. They almost expect you to treat them like crap because, hey, they treated you like crap. So you walk away and feel like you had a real psychological dig. I know that sounds cruel. But I don't care.

I mean, like, limousines. I think all that stuff's over the top. None of it impresses me at all. But for high school reunions you have to play the part. So I'm gonna get the most massive limousine I can find. You take at least two girls with you, and make sure you pick two obvious bimbos. And you go back home . . . you have to make the point. One girl is on each arm, and you say 'Gosh, I'm sorry I can't stay any longer, I have to go to the Grammys.' Then you drive away. You have to do it right, or it's not worth doing at all. Do it where you're slightly rubbing their nose in it, but not enough to be tactless.

It sounds like DeLand pissed you off in a big way.

Hey look, some people say that I've got a chip on my shoulder, but rock and roll was started by people with chips on their shoulders. It's the tradition. It's better than being very safe and boring and being conservative, coffee table.

(*He has recovered. His British accent is back in place. He gets up from the couch and walks about the office.*)

What did you want to be when you were in high school? I don't get the impression that you had this

burning desire to be a rock star.
No, my desire was to be a star. Not a star in the superficial sense. I wanted to be a writer. I wanted to be heavyweight champion of the world. I wanted to be a marine biologist. (*laughs*)Yeah, I did want to be a writer, a journalist. But I was obviously insane and I didn't know my head from a hole in the ground. One can either go into music or journalism; you go either way and grind your axes.

My first recognized gift as a child was writing, and I'm still, if I may say so, quite a good writer. I do lots of writing which will be published someday. I was editor of the school paper and stuff like that. Managing editor of the school paper.

So you did well in school?
I did good in stuff I was interested in. I never applied myself. I didn't have to try. Things I wasn't interested in I did badly in. My sophomore year in high school I did badly, 'cause I actually tripped out on the fact I was in high school. You know, 'Hey, I'm free ... I'm in high school!' I've been very lucky. I believe I have a guardian angel or a protective force watching me, cause sometimes I've just got so close to the edge of things. And just played with the fact that I'm on the edge. But I've come out OK. I mean, sophomore year in high school is a year that really could change your life. No college is going to take you seriously ... 'just look at those grades, young man!' But I just didn't care.

Did you seriously mess up that year?
Well, I was already fucked up. I've always been sort of fucked up. I didn't need drugs for that. There were too many things going on in my head.

Did they send you to a shrink?
Yeah, and I used to have fun fucking with his head. Adults, if you're not careful, will always try to lay this trip on you like, 'No, you don't understand ... ' And you know perfectly well the problem is that *they* don't understand the deal. You gotta suspect people who want to get into other people's heads for a living, when you can just go down the road, go into a bar, have a couple of drinks, and do it for free.

(He lapses back into a high school, American accent.)

I was into mushrooms. I never got into pot. I was a good kid in that respect. I never saw the need. When you're sort of out there already, you're trying to pull it back in, not push it out there more.

So what happened after that alienated sophomore year?
I'm an extremist. That state of existence just bored me, so I decided to take some classes that interested me, and get some good grades in school.

God! Why are you taking me back to all these places I don't wanna go!

You just said you wanted to go back there.
Yeah, but only for five or six minutes. You know, just let the guy change the tyre and get on the road again. I'm sorry, did I stumble into the wrong place? No Terence, remember, you went to school here. Oh, did I? Nice to see you. Do I know you? Oh, we were in homeroom together for four years! I'm sorry, I have to go, well wasn't this a coincidence. I didn't know you guys were actually having this high school reunion. Well, so sorry, I'm on my way to the Grammys. See ya later. I'll wave to you from the television.

But you did get out of DeLand, and it was OK, you got into college ...
Mis-take! My father got me to go. I was bored, I dropped out. I went to the University of Central Florida on a journalism scholarship. They didn't teach me anything I didn't think I already knew, they were almost messing me up. Institutions as a whole tend to be designed to take individuality away from one. To try to give you a nice corporate mentality that allows you to function inside the greater society. I've always been a square peg, I'll never fit into a round hole, why should I make myself do that? Although I succumbed to that when I joined the Army. I actually allowed people to brainwash me into thinking, 'Yeah, Terence, maybe you *do* need to settle down into a groove and be a contributing, functioning member of a responsible community.' All that sort of bollocks that you read about in Christmas cards and Norman Rockwell.

And mom, well, she didn't want me to go. I was the first baby, and they never want you to leave the

house. But she thought, well, maybe the Army will make a man of me. That was her consolation. Well, if anyone knows what a man is, I wish they would please let me know. I don't know if I am a man now. What is this concept that wars were fought over? I am a man. What the hell is that?

(D'Arby is very agitated. He goes back over to the couch and sits back, crossing his arms and legs.)

Who did you write for?

I used to do stuff for the paper in DeLand. **The Deland Sun News.**

(He yawns, loudly.)

Hey, I don't want to talk about that stuff, really. Let's talk about music.

Were you on the newspaper staff? What kinds of things did you write?

Anything I wanted, really. Dogs chasing me down the street, and why the hell doesn't the city keep these dogs from chasing me. What is this, a jungle or a community here? The maniacal ravings of a 16 year old. You're a kid, you write to see your byline in a paper. You do it for free because you love it. I'd do this for free, I'd perform music for free, except there are actually people out there called moguls who pay you a fortune to do it. So you think, wow, if you're going to be so stupid as to give me a fortune to do this, well . . . I'll take it.

Did you start off by singing in church?

Yeah. That's original, ain't it. I, uh, really . . . *(suddenly)* Nah, I didn't sing in the church. At least I'm saying I didn't for the moment. It's a bit of a cliché, that. Look, let's talk about music.

OK. That was why I asked you about singing in church . . .

I don't want to talk about music from . . . well, you know what I mean. Look, so I sang a bit in church. You were a kid, big fat ladies with, like, *massive* tits would come give you a hug and smother you with affection. Such warmth! They would rub your head, and you figure, well if this is what I get, well, fine. I'll keep doing it. It's your first indication that maybe I'm doing something that maybe I should look more seriously into. They always go on about how I got into music because of the aesthetic nature of man communicating with his brother. Bollocks! I got into music because I wanted to get laid. I can either shoot a basketball through a hoop semi-successfully, or I can take a guitar, sit under an oak tree, strum a few chords, pretend I'm Bob Dylan and attract the attention of the girls. Once I saw this worked, I said, I gotta keep up with this. Simple. I got into music to get laid.

Look, you're a kid, you got a big Afro, you're pale, people think you're cute. Hmmmmph! I looked like a chipmunk. If I think back on it, I was like this cute kid with hazel eyes and these massive chubby cheeks. You get up, you sing, you bring the house down, people like you. I don't remember the first time I sang, for some reason I don't. I remember Kennedy being shot, but not Martin Luther King, though that was six, seven years later. Don't ask me why. We choose our moments. I'd sing, girls would move up to the front, I thought I was the cat's meow. Some people think I still do. Well this is my problem, man, to work out.

(D'Arby stares off. His manner has turned combative and surly. Time to stop talking about church.)

Were you in a band in Florida?

I had never been in a band in my life until I moved to Europe.

So what were the circumstances of your performing when you were younger? Did you do a solo thing with a guitar in school, or in clubs?

Ehhhhhh . . . this conversation is like, uh, bending my sense of consciousness at the moment. You know those times where you think you're going crazy? Those times are becoming more and more frequent for me.

But really, I don't want to talk about this because, like . . . you know. Let's talk about music. Just music. Well, really, as a matter of fact, we could talk about anything. At the moment you're pulling me back to a place where I really don't want to go at the moment. When I decide to talk to someone I try to open myself up, and it's not a beautiful thing. Sometimes what you're talking about, what makes you feel passionate, reopens channels that you want to close for a certain period of time. Right now, you're reopening a past that I don't

ARIEL

TRIUMPH

particularly want to go to. For whatever reason, God only knows.

I'm really tired. I'm sorry about that. I'm not as coherent as I usually am.

I couldn't figure out why D'Arby was acting so touchy and rude. Was his past that difficult a subject? I hadn't asked him anything terribly personal, or more confrontational than what you'd find in a **Smash Hits** interview (the **Smash Hits** interviewer would've probably already asked D'Arby about his sexual preferences and the names of his last eight girlfriends!). So what was the problem? I decided the best thing to do was to ask him one or two more questions, then quickly bring our meeting to a close. Hopefully, he would be in a better mood for talking the following day, when I was scheduled to accompany him on his rounds of TV interviews.

What was it like when you finally started singing with a band?
Why should people know how I felt! (*explodes angrily*) We know too much in this fucking world. We don't think. I've never seen a generation so afraid to think in my life. We can pick up **USA Today** and see everything put down in little graphs. My first band? (*calms down*)It was a sense of power I never felt before. It wasn't like singing in church, and having to suppose that little girls were liking you. It was actually seeing it. Having knickers hit you in the face when you were on stage. The joy of getting paid for something you would do for free. You were getting a chance to sleep until 12 o'clock in the day, wake up, take things at your own pace. I'd never had that in my life before, ever. You had your own gang. There was that camaraderie. I've never liked guys, I've never got along with guys. Up to this day, the only time I've ever got along with guys is when we're together working on music. Almost every friend I've ever had has been a woman. And it was sort of like, I've got this male gang I belong to, we've got this thing going, and it's real good.

D'Arby talks for a little while about his experiences as an up-and-coming rock singer in his first band in Germany. His mood, tone and accent fluctuate wildly. After a few minutes more, I suggest that since he's tired, we stop and pick up again later and talk about the music and the production of his album. D'Arby nods wearily, and says a few final words:

Look, I'm not doing anything different from what Jerry Lee Lewis was doing, or what the rappers are doing now. It's the same shit. Rock is about adopting an attitude and pose. It's sticking your chest out and having a bit of fucking fun. It pisses me off how so many people write without a fucking sense of humour. I'm milking this. I'm having fun. I'm an artist through and through. But once you've made your record, your work's done. What do I do in the meantime? I'm bored! Nothing pisses me off more than people who can't appreciate irony. I like doing shit that pisses people off. I don't know why. I guess it's part of my nature.

Laverty knocked on the door and came in to tell D'Arby it was time to go to dinner. He said goodbye, hurriedly, and walked off, presumably to find Claudine. When he was gone, Laverty asked me if things had gone smoothly, and I told her the truth: no. 'He's very tired,' she said, apologetically. 'And he's very shy. It takes him a long time to feel comfortable with people. I'm just now getting to know him.' She paused a moment. 'He's a very intelligent, unique and special person.'

The H

chapter 3

ustler

The

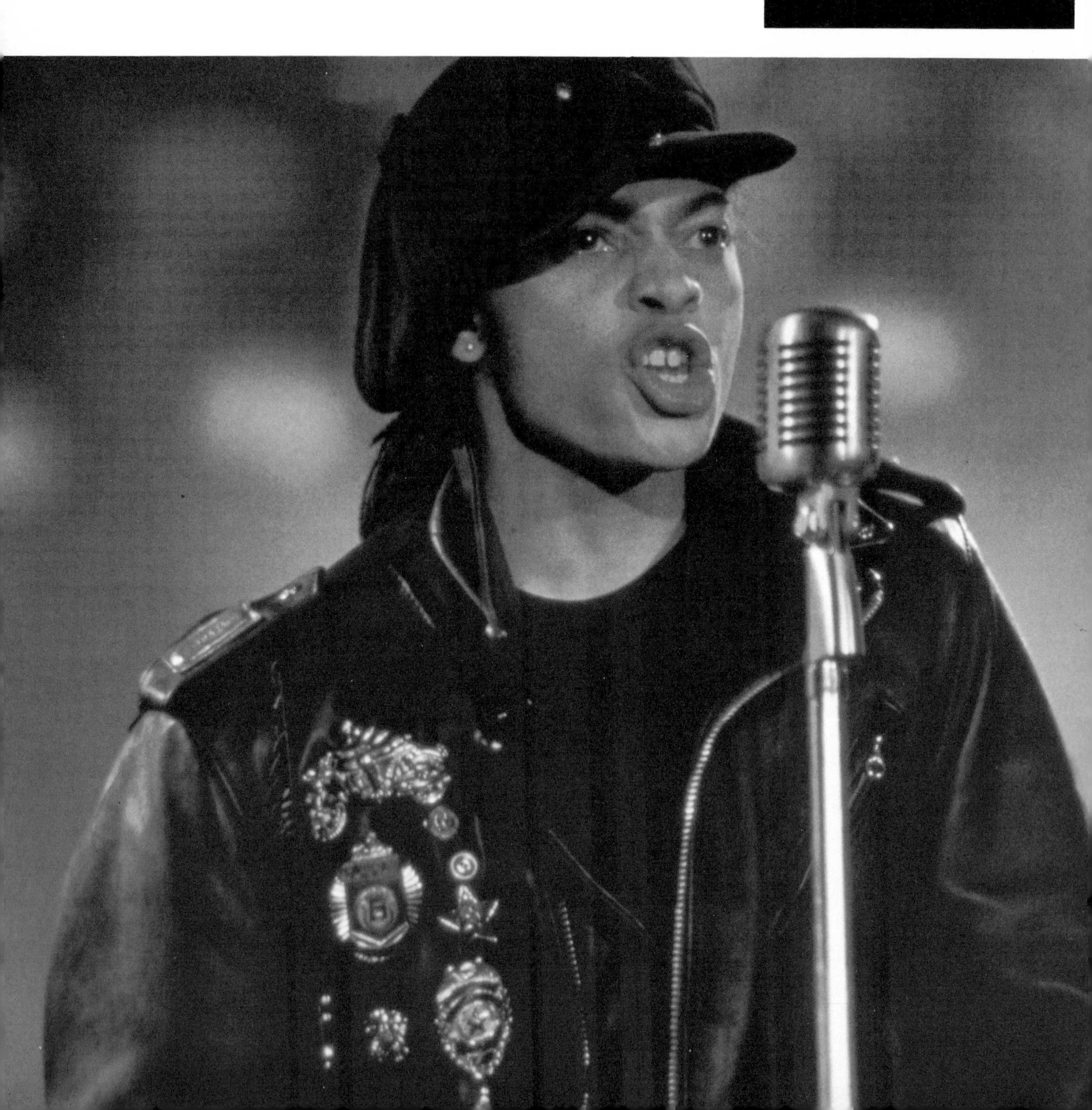

Hustler

forthcoming live tour. There's nothing remarkable about this exchange, except what's left out of it: criticism of the USA, talk about discrimination, politics and sex. The Terence Trent D'Arby who likes to 'piss people off'. Neither the presenter nor D'Arby says the word black.

The following afternoon, I meet Laverty, Claudine and D'Arby at the studios of MTV on the west side of Manhattan. D'Arby's scheduled to do a short interview with one of the presenters, and then record some promotional spots that will be shown over and over again during the next few months.

MTV, the major music network in the US, is the headquarters of mainstream rock and roll. Their core audience is under 25, white, and suburban. More males than females. You won't see any independent-label or local band's videos on MTV's regular programmes, and when a black act makes it on to the screen, it's a singular event (Michael Jackson; Run DMC; Sade; Tracy Chapman).

Playing billiards in the studio lounge as he waits to be called in for his spot, D'Arby appears infinitely more at ease than he did yesterday, and he looks like a rock star. He's wearing the same black clothes, but he's left the RayBans behind. Now, when he smiles, those huge, trademark hazel eyes shine like amber beads. The press is right: D'Arby's charming. The MTV director finally arrives: they're ready for Terence. Our party troops into the recording area, an enormous room that contains two sets. One is a recreation of an old sixties-style hippie parlour, the kind of funky San Francisco pad you'd imagine the Jefferson Airplane would have lived in then. There's a threadbare Salvation Army sofa, an old rag rug, and an assortment of raffish odds-and-ends; antique posters, funny hats, old licence plates on the wall. Tacky, whimsical decor like this used to be a statement of non-conformity, of the alternative, 'rock and roll' lifestyle. Now, it's a backdrop on nationwide television.

D'Arby is being recorded on the other set, a Cadillac-modern tableau of plasticized neon and chrome that's made to look like a booth in a 1950s diner. He sits opposite the presenter – a six-foot tanned Viking with shoulder length hair, and the five minute interview begins. The content is pure music-biz chit-chat; the presenter begins by welcoming D'Arby to the US, mentioning his fabulous success in the UK, and asking D'Arby what his plans are here. D'Arby, in a soft and polite voice, talks about how his record is doing, and about his

'We're after simultaneous development: Black, rock and roll, and pop,' D'Arby's CBS product manager Steve Berkowitz had explained to me over the phone earlier that day. I had phoned Berkowitz because, as product manager, he's in charge of coordinating Terence Trent D'Arby's US marketing strategy. 'We're hitting all the markets at once. So far it's been a dream development. The first single, "If You Let Me Stay", was in the Top 20 of the black charts, and Top 100 pop. "Wishing Well" is going great. It's all very well timed. A dream development.'

Berkowitz only recently started working for CBS in New York, but he has obviously mastered Black Rock company-speak. Like most CBS personnel, he was reluctant to be interviewed, and it took a bit of arm-twisting to get him to answer some simple questions. Since his responses were so carefully edited, I assumed they quite accurately represented the CBS 'party line' on the selling of D'Arby:

I've heard that D'Arby is a top priority act, and that CBS is spending an unusually large amount of money to get his career started here. Is that so?

(Berkowitz) There is a more than average size promotional budget for this artist because of his proven success in another marketplace.

Is CBS underwriting D'Arby's forthcoming US tour?

There is tour support from the company, but the tour is making money. Boston's dates are sold out, New York is very close.

What is your target audience for Terence Trent D'Arby?

As I said, we're after everybody. The album broke in the small record shops in Boston and San Francisco who are aware of what's going on in Europe. And on trendsetting AOR stations.

I'd say that the audience is split about 50–50 male and female. It's a racially mixed audience. Terence is breaking now. He's moving into the Top 30 album chart, the black Top 20. The album is close to going gold. For a first record by a new act in the US, it has been tremendously successful. We're pleased.

And, you know, I think that the public really *wants* to like Terence . . .

Berkowitz's comments come to mind now as I watch D'Arby moving like a consummate pro through his MTV paces. Apparently, CBS intended to duplicate the marketing strategy that had worked for D'Arby in England. D'Arby, like Sade several years before, was being aimed straight at the American pop market. If the black fans jumped in as well, the more the merrier, but the major promotional push wasn't in that direction. D'Arby was getting exactly what he wanted from CBS: the opportunity to make it in America as pop star. Even Prince had to spend years on the r&b circuit before he got that chance. This was a major coup for Terence Trent D'Arby.

Every victory, however, has its price. The D'Arby sitting in the pseudo-diner booth exchanging pleasantries with the Viking presenter about his recent Grammy nomination (for 'Best New Artist') is certainly a different D'Arby from the one who'd supplied half the magazines in Britain with controversial copy a few short months ago. This D'Arby says no to most press interviews, and has chosen to appear only in controlled media situations, just like a certain US president. And I wonder: Is this D'Arby's idea, or CBS's, or both?

After the five minute take, the director asks D'Arby to re-do the interview in shorter format. I walk over to talk to Claudine, who is standing in the back, far enough away so she can't hear D'Arby, but can see him.

Claudine Martinet, I'd found out since yesterday's interview, is originally from Andorra, a tiny country tucked between France and Spain. She speaks several languages, is married to an English musician, and for the last few years, together with another woman partner, has run her own publicity company in London specializing in black artists. My sources in London told me that she is a rare breed – a good, intelligent publicist who gives an extra measure for acts she believes in, even if there's not a lot of money in the gig. D'Arby, apparently, is her first big-league client, and he's quickly become a special, full-time job. Publicists, even personal ones, rarely go on tour with their clients, handle all their arrangements, and oversee their schedules. But that's what Martinet is doing.

'Yes, it is true,' Martinet says, 'Terry sees more of me than anyone else, especially when we're on the road like this.' She's still keeping a concerned, protective eye on D'Arby as we speak, although she's so poised and polite one hardly notices her attention is distracted.

Is D'Arby difficult to work with? I ask.

No, she says, but he's difficult to get to know. He's very guarded with strangers. 'He's sensitive, and extremely intelligent. He's curious about everything, and he reads constantly.'

I ask her what sort of writing interests D'Arby, and she mentions a book that she passed along to him, **The Gospel According to Woman**, which is a feminist re-interpretation of Christian theology. D'Arby, she says, is fascinated by the book's analysis of how Christianity was used to control and manipulate woman's position in society.

That's just one example, Martinet continues. D'Arby reads biography and history, and is obsessed at the moment with the music of Stravinsky. He's being exposed to so many new things now, she tells me. Music, literature, art. And he's eating it up.

When the final take is finished, D'Arby walks back into the studio lounge. Laverty and Martinet go out to make phone calls, he says a quick goodbye, and we head for the next stop: an interview with Rona Elliot, the music correspondent of the Today Show.

'So, what's your favourite Marvin Gaye LP?'

'If you want to get laid, **Let's Get It On** is the one,' quips Rona Elliot. Elliot, a wisecracking Jewish mother-type in her mid-forties, is letting D'Arby interview *her*. And he's eating out of her hand.

'Who else did you get into, Rona?'

'Joni Mitchell, Dylan . . . '

'Dylan,' snorts D'Arby. 'Man, he just wanted to pose with the telecaster like everybody else.'

'Well,' she says, 'Rock and roll has room for every point of view.'

'Wehhhll,' challenges D'Arby, in his best English accent. 'Is there room for every point of view in America today?' (Meaning: Is there room for mine?)

'We'll see,' retorts Rona Elliot.

After listening to Elliot and D'Arby go on for several minutes, I realize what D'Arby meant yesterday when he kept insisting he wanted to talk about 'music, just music'. He didn't mean his own music, but that of *other performers*. He's having a good time now with Elliot, because they're two fans talking shop.

When they settle down and start the real on-the-air interview, D'Arby's back in his best quotable form. He cracks jokes about Willard Scott, the Today Show co-host. In his thickest British accent, he talks about the 'dichotomy' of the Pisces astrological sign, and how it is manifest in his personality. Elliot asks him about growing up in the church and his musical influences, and he doesn't baulk at the question. 'If the gospel influence is still in my music today, it's totally subconscious,' he maintains.

I make a note of the best one-liners:

'I'm a big fan of Muhammad Ali, and, like him, I know the value of a good quote.'

'Michael Jackson is the Fred Astaire of my generation.'

'I got into rock and roll to get laid. Having a big mouth helps.'

Elliot is ecstatic. She knows this is going to come out as a great interview when it's edited. In the flesh, D'Arby's withdrawn; in front of a camera, he's incandescent. When he's the centre of attention D'Arby comes alive.

And he's really got a sense of dramatic timing. At one point Elliot gets serious, looks deeply into his eyes, and asks him if he's afraid of anything. D'Arby quickly says, 'No, I fear nothing,' then falls silent, and stares off moodily into the distance. Finally he adds, almost in a whisper. 'OK . . . I fear losing my head.'

Does he really mean that, or is it a great performance? It's difficult to tell. But later, when Elliot asks him if he's emotionally open and honest as an artist, or if he protects himself, D'Arby says something rather revealing. 'I believe that if you're going to open yourself to old hurts and angers, if those wounds have to come open . . . the place to do it is on stage.'

After the recording is finished, they keep talking. D'Arby wants to know what other rock people Elliot has interviewed – did she know Marvin Gaye? Yes, she once met him. D'Arby laughs and says something about the 'Jesus/pussy' dichotomy of having a church background; as if that was

something he's thought about a lot. Elliot asks him what records he's been listening to, and D'Arby demurs: do you *really* want to know? Well, OK: Bartok, Stravinsky, Erik Satie. Then Elliot asks him one last question: are both your parents black? D'Arby shrugs. My mother is black, he tells her. And the father who raised me is black.

Since D'Arby had finished the TV interviews, I suggested now was a good time to have a cup of tea and finish off our interview from yesterday.

Claudine takes over. 'We have no more time.'

Then tomorrow?

'I really don't think so,' she says. 'You can call me if you want.'

Her manner indicates that there's no point in pushing it. So I say one more thing to D'Arby: I explain that I would also like to interview some people who are close to him, so that their comments and observations can help to present a complete picture in the profile I am writing. Is there anyone he can suggest I speak to about his career? A teacher, another musician, a friend?

D'Arby laughs. 'Anybody you can find, you can talk to them,' he snaps, in a tone that suggests 'You'll be lucky.'

He and Claudine disappear, leaving Laverty, once again, apologetic. 'He just doesn't feel like giving out information about himself at this point. That's why he's doing so few interviews. He doesn't feel he has any more to say.'

I am on the verge of asking why he bothered to come here, in that case, but instead, I ask Laverty to verify some of the information D'Arby gave me during yesterday's interview.

She says she's not even sure if Terence Trent D'Arby is his real name.

The next day I called Claudine at the hotel, but there was no answer. I sat down with my tapes and my notes, and wondered what to do next. D'Arby was certainly an intriguing character, a bundle of contradictions. And the politics and machinery of his US marketing campaign was a story all by itself. But I only had small fragments of the puzzle. If I was really going to go ahead and do a proper profile I needed more information.

On tape, D'Arby had been forthcoming about his teenage years for a while; and he had lots to say – to me, MTV and Rona Elliot – about his career today. But how did he get from there to here? There was one period of his life that remained particularly unclear; the years in West Germany.

D'Arby, according to his account, was sent to Germany by the US Army, and, through a series of circumstances, ended up deserting his unit to be the lead singer in a funk/rock band. It was through this band that he met his current manager, a mysterious figure known only as 'KP'. KP had promoted D'Arby's career energetically until finally he got him a record deal in England. Here's how D'Arby recounted that period:

(TTD) My band was Germans. We were hard, we were wicked! We were playing some amalgamation of funk and rock which I'd never even heard, never even listened to until I got to Europe. Our own stuff, all original. Which is weird. I envy guys that know 400 tunes they can just jam with anything. Anyway, it was Germans who turned me on to funk music. I'd always listened more to rock, old r&b, country, jazz and folk.

How did you find this band, or how did they find you?

I stumbled into this guy in a music shop in Frankfurt when he was buying a bass guitar, and I asked him if he knew of any band that I could sing with, because I'm a singer. And he said, 'Are you good?' and I said yeah. I hadn't sung in years, and I was talking bollocks as I usually do, just trying to drive my way into a situation. And this guy walked in after he said that, and said, 'I know a band that needs a singer, because I'm the singer and I'm leaving.' Ha! My life is like that.

I hadn't sung in years, didn't even know if I could still hold a tune. He set me up with an audition, and the rest, well, it wasn't history, but it was something. It was a start.

You went AWOL from the Army in order to be with this band?

Yeah, sort of. I was having deep, deep problems with the military. I got the record for Article 15s. It's like an official reprimand that's punishable. I was in supply. My great intellect was obviously used to great effect there. Now, see, that's something that, when you see it in cold print you say, 'Wow, what an arrogant bastard.' But I don't care. I'm an extremist. Sometimes I say nothing for two or three days, other times it's like I'm on speed, and I can't stop.

Did you have to hide from the Army?

Yeah, I was in hiding. It was really romantic. A fugitive on the run. Wanted. It was brilliant. It was serious mythology, rock and roll, rebelling against the establishment. Going out and hiding.

They never caught me, nah, I turned myself in. For the legend, we should probably write it that I was caught, beaten, they dragged me back in. But that wasn't what happened.

Anyway it was a real romantic scene. Every gig, I wondered, well, could this be my last gig for years? Especially since in a lot of the clubs we played in, GIs would come to these gigs. It was frightening, but at the same time, the tension ... well, when I went out there, I always believed nothing could happen to me. I was protected by some unseen force. I always believed that. I think if you believe strongly enough in anything, that makes it true.

What made you turn yourself in?

I was starting to like this thing too much. I decided if I wanted to continue to do it, I had to gamble. Take the chance that I could go to prison, because I knew the Army was going to try to send me there. They wanted to send me to prison for five years, and the odds looked heavily against me.

Did you go see a lawyer?

Definitely! I went back to the Army with the lawyer. And they told me, 'Yeah, we're gonna be fair with you, Terence.' Then, after the lawyer left, they laid into me. It was sort of a really heavy scene. This was in Hanau, Frankfurt, Germany. So I had to get me a real good ol' New York Jewish lawyer.

They're expensive. Where did you get the money to do that?

I got the money. You know, you break into people's homes, steal their TV sets.

You had some backing at this point?

My guardian angel. When they watch over you, you don't mess around. Like fans and stuff, when they knew I was in trouble, they sent money to help. That's basically it. Fans would send money. Really romantic, those days. Obviously, in the future, when I write about it, I'll make it more romantic. About how they handcuffed me, and took me away and all that. Next question.

Were you, in fact court-martialled?

They did put the screws on me! Look, I had a trial, I was court-martialled at the trial, but the sentence was deferred. I would've been sent away for five years to prison. The trial took a long time, it was a big deal, because all my witnesses had been intimidated. I was being used as an example because there had been some corruption in the unit, and morale had fallen very badly, so therefore, I became the kingpin. A lot of the troops were looking at what was happening to me to see how much I would get away with.

Were they accusing you of anything besides going AWOL?

Just complete conduct unbecoming a soldier. Unbecoming a member of the human race. It was getting quite heavy. Like, they'll find something. Maybe two months before you joined the unit somebody stole some money from the first sergeant's desk. So they'll pin that on you as well.

Did they have witnesses?

They're the army. Say a guy might be up for sergeant in a few months. So he figures, well, I'll help the Army now with this trial, then when my name comes up for promotion ... Fucking corrupt. It can be, I should say.

At the same time, since I had such a naive sense of fate and destiny, I'd be sitting there thinking, I wonder what it would be like to be in prison? It didn't really dawn on me that I could be spending the next five years of my life there, really. You could come out like a waterhose, Terence, and have to use Preparation H or something. I sort of felt, well, I just didn't think about it. Five years. 1700 days.

I got out at the last minute. You

I know what happened? The odds were greatly stacked against me. They deliberated for hours with my life hanging in the balance. Sometimes it's something simple like one of these guys got laid the night before, or he had a good golf game, and he's just in the mood to say, 'Why don't we let this kid out? We've got 500 trying to get in.' So they just kicked me out. Then, they try to make you believe your life is ruined, that no one will want you because you're an outcast from the Army. Can you see me going to some record company and them saying to me, 'Wow, Terence, we really like your stuff, but you know, you were kicked out of the Army . . . '

In one interview, you said that you had a nervous breakdown in the Army, and that's why they let you out.

Well, I was going to the mental hygiene facility. And they were sort of saying, yeah, this guy is losing his mind. Since I've come out of there, I've become more fragmented. And my handwriting changed after the Army. Something deep within me changed.

I met KP after all this took place.

Was it shortly after that you started going over to England?

Yeah.

What made you hook up with KP?

I thought he looked cool. That was it. We were very wary of each other but we liked each other at the same time. We've fought every day of our lives since then. But I know him, and I trust him.

If anyone had an insight into D'Arby's transition from disaffected GI to British rock star, it had to be KP. Marilyn Laverty had mentioned that KP was in New York now, but I hadn't seen him at the CBS offices, or at the television tapings – D'Arby was accompanied only by Claudine. Laverty had promised to put me in touch with KP next week, but I knew that the whole D'Arby entourage was leaving for Los Angeles the next day.

KP's company was called PARC. I looked in the Manhattan phone book; it was listed. Even though it was Saturday afternoon, it was worth a try.

A sleepy voice answered on the first ring.

'Ja?'

'Is this KP?'

'Ja. Who is this?'

I explained. KP invited me over.

The PARC office is also KP's New York base; my call had woken him up. But by the time I arrived, he was full of energy. KP appeared to be in his mid-forties; bubbly, elfin, with an unstoppable grin. He led me into a room with a couch and a stereo system.

KP – his full name is Klaus Pieter Schleinitz – told me that he met D'Arby when he was a press officer for the record company Ariola International in Munich,

MTV

around 1982. D'Arby was in a group called Touch that was playing in the clubs around Frankfurt and Munich. 'It was a good band, but it lacked orientation,' KP said.

What were his impressions of D'Arby then?

'He was figuring out what was going on. He still is.'

KP bounded over to his stereo set, and asked me if I knew he had his own record label in Germany? He pulled out a copy of an album by Kevin Ayers, an idiosyncratic and definitely un-commercial English songwriter, explaining that

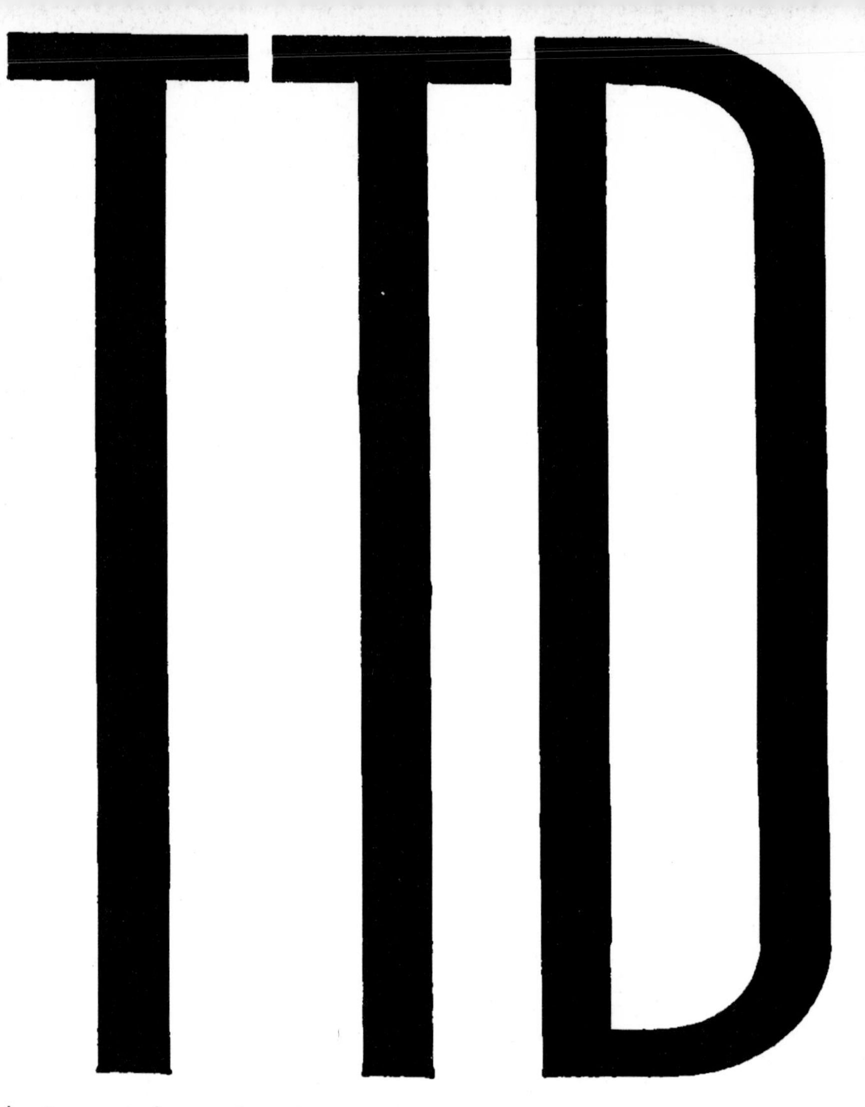

he put Ayers' record out in Germany, along with several albums by a Jamaican reggae band called Chalice he discovered during one of his many trips to the West Indies. He suddenly interjected:

'But you should hear the Lee Perry dub mix of "Wishing Well"!'

He put it on the turntable, explaining that, back in the old days in Germany, he and D'Arby used to sit around into the small hours, listening to Perry's ganja-surrealist productions. And they would imagine what it would be like to work in the studio with him someday. Now, they know.

'Wishing Well' began to ooze through KP's speakers, in 100% pure Jamaican re-channelled distortion. It sounded fantastic.

'Only available in the UK,' KP smiled proudly. 'Collector's item.'

When the record finished, KP returned to the subject of D'Arby. 'Terry is very strong, he sees things very clear. Did you know that at least 50% of the songs on the album were recorded in demo form when we were still in Germany? His music is able to motivate everybody, everybody can get into it.'

As his manager, I asked him, what do you think about CBS's plans for breaking D'Arby in America?

KP didn't answer directly. He said that he was a great admirer of Jake Riviera, Elvis Costello's manager. And, like Riviera, he liked to be fluid, flexible. 'We aim for every audience. I've always told Terry, if you go to the US, you don't want to be marketed as a black act. We've tried to avoid that.

'CBS . . . it's a brilliant company if you use it right,' KP chuckled conspiratorially. 'Yetnikoff (the president of CBS) and all those old guys, they can still see talent.'

KP went back over to the stereo. He told me that he was still developing new acts in addition to D'Arby, and that he had some work-in-progress – would I mind giving it a listen? Just then, we were interrupted by the entrance of a young woman. She burst into his office like sunshine through the clouds, and KP stood up, ran over to her, and gave her a big hug. 'Sherry!' he exclaimed. 'How are you!'

Sherry was dark-skinned, tall and a bit plump, and wore a long skirt. She told KP she didn't want to interrupt him, and that she'd see him back at the hotel. Then said good-bye, beaming from ear to ear. Where had I seen that smile before . . .?

KP, who was that girl? She looked familiar.

'Of course. That was Terry's sister.'

D'Arby's *sister*?!

'Ja, she flew up from Florida to see him while he was in New York. It's a huge family. There are others somewhere out in, where, New Jersey? We're all going out there tonight. It's a big group, but Terry is very close to them, he keeps in touch. They are good people. When you meet them, you understand Terry much better.'

chapter 4

Favours

on
ite

Favourite Son

After the media day with D'Arby, and my talk with KP, I returned to the **Village Voice** office to consult the editor, Kit Rachlis. Even though I knew I was risking my assignment, I told Rachlis straight off that D'Arby had been difficult, and that I wasn't sure I had a story. Rachlis listened carefully as I gave him a summary of the interview at Black Rock, and the scenes in MTV and at the Today Show. Then I recounted the CBS publicity department's manipulations, and D'Arby's diffident parting suggestion to 'find whoever I could' to talk to.

I described in detail D'Arby's emotionally-charged responses to the queries about his adolescence, because they had intrigued me more than anything else he'd said or done. The subject seemed to touch some very deep, vulnerable place. I couldn't stop wondering what had happened to D'Arby to make him so hurt and angry that, even today, it bothered him to remember those days. Had D'Arby been in jail, or involved in some violence? Is that why D'Arby and CBS were so paranoid and so reluctant to provide concrete facts about his past?

Then I told Rachlis about bumping into Sherry – D'Arby? – in KP's office. KP had said that Sherry 'came up from Florida' to see her brother. That suggested that the family still lived there, perhaps in the town that D'Arby had mentioned in the interview – DeLand.

I was pretty sure D'Arby was telling the truth, that his mother and dad were living in that small Florida town. But even if D'Arby's family wasn't there, someone must remember him at his old high school. Once I got to DeLand, D'Arby's trail would be easy to find.

Rachlis suggested that I call Directory Enquiries in DeLand, and see if there were any D'Arbys in town. He handed me the phone; the Florida operator said that there were two Darbys – a Mr RC Darby, and another named James Benjamin!

'So,' Rachlis chuckled, 'When are you leaving for Florida?'

The plane was three hours late leaving New York. When it finally touched down in Orlando, Florida, home of Disney World, the sun was beginning to sink, and so were my spirits. I still had about two hours of driving ahead of me, and it would be dark before I reached my hotel.

For the first half-hour, I drove along the multi-laned motorway that circles downtown Orlando, a fantasy land of gold and silver-toned glass and steel skyscrapers. New money, Disney World development. If Terence Trent D'Arby did grow up in this area, Orlando would've been the nearest big city. D'Arby would have lived here around 10 to 12

D'Arby's home town, DeLand, Florida.

TRIUMPH
Velocette

years ago, when all this development was just beginning.

On the radio, local news bulletins announced the forthcoming arrival of still another major industry to the Orlando area: Universal Studios. The film and TV company was about to move a big chunk of its production facilities out here from Los Angeles. But the environment was unprepossessing: the air felt moist and heavy, and the city sits on a flat, semi-swamp, miles away from the ocean. Before the new money, and the Disney/Universal boom, when D'Arby lived nearby, what was Orlando like?

As I drove on, the traffic gradually diminished. There were no longer buildings and houses alongside the road, only dense woods. Then night fell. The air suddenly changed, and started to smell of the countryside. The road signs indicated that water was all around: Lake Monroe, Blue Springs State Park; Lake Helen. At last a sign appeared marked DeLand.

By now it was nine o'clock, and most of the petrol stations and shopping centres along this local road were dark and closed. I'd been travelling since early in the morning, and I was tired and hungry. At last I came to a crossroads: just off to the right was a 7–11 (a US chain of grocery shops). God bless America, I muttered to myself, and pulled in. Was I on the right road to DeLand?

'You're in it,' answered the assistant.

He sold me a map for two dollars. 'Two bucks too much, if you ask me,' he commented, to nobody in particular.

I'd expected, at the very least, a suburban wasteland. Or a tense, narrow-minded Southern hamlet. A place that would utterly depress me and instantly reveal the sources of Terence Trent D'Arby's alienation. Instead, on the morning of the following day, I found myself driving through peaceful, oak-lined streets in a pretty turn-of-the-century university town. 'Welcome to DeLand – the Athens of Northern Florida,' said a local billboard. In the centre of town was the campus of Stetson University, named after the millionaire hat baron who gave the school its endowment. Stetson's main building, a Victorian mansion flanked by a line of palm trees, looked as though it belonged in Hollywood.

Like most American high schools, DeLand High School, Terence Trent D'Arby's alleged alma mater, was sprawling, dreary, and institutional. And huge – it appeared to have enough room for several thousand students. There were several low grey-brown and brick-red structures, connected by a series of concrete pathways lined on both sides with steel lockers for books and personal belongings. Although the buildings were square and dull, it was a nice touch to have the hallways and corridors outdoors – one big advantage of going to school in sunny Florida.

The electronic bell rang to announce the change of classes as I walked into the complex. All at once the pathways filled with laughing and chatting students. They were dressed casually, in Jeans and t-shirts and sneakers. Neither rich nor poor. Some black faces, not many. DeLand was like any suburban small-town high school; average, and solidly middle-class. Mostly nice kids, not too 'tough' – this didn't look like a leather-and-switchblade scene. I didn't see teachers or monitors patrolling the campus (a common practice in American high schools). The DeLand students were apparently well-behaved, and didn't require constant adult scrutiny. In fact, I got all the way to the principal's office and no one bothered to ask who the stranger was.

The principal's secretary was busy; her desk was covered with papers. I approached her sheepishly – suppose this wasn't the right high school? I took a deep breath, and asked if the school had any record of a former student named Terence Trent . . .

'Well of *course*!' she exclaimed, before I had a chance to finish the sentence. She continued, matter-of-factly, 'Down here we all know him as Terry Darby, His mother is a teacher in the junior high school, and his father is a preacher with

TTD

his own church in town. You mean you haven't read all the articles they've been writing about the Darbys in the newspaper?'

I asked her what newspaper. She looked at me as if I'd just wandered in from Mars.

'Why, the **DeLand Sun News**. They've run quite a few stories about Terry and his family, and about how he credits the DeLand teachers with all his success in music. We have some very fine music teachers here, you know, and . . . '

I could hardly believe what I was hearing. Not only was D'Arby indeed from DeLand, but he was a town hero, local boy makes good. And, apparently, he'd been giving a rather different speech to the people from his home town than to reporters in New York. When the secretary paused, I mentioned that one of the reasons I'd come to DeLand in search of D'Arby – Darby's – past was that he had described his years in this high school with such bitterness.

She said she couldn't imagine why he'd feel that way. Then she went to the school library and came back with a copy of the **DeLand Athenian**, the yearbook of D'Arby's graduating class of 1979. (A yearbook, or annual, is an American high school tradition: a large bound volume of 100 or so pages that contains reminiscences of the school year, group pictures of all the clubs and sports teams, and individual photos of the teachers and students.) The secretary flipped to the pages that had pictures of 'Terry'. And there he was: skinny, shorter, a bit goofy-looking, wearing wire-rimmed glasses.

'This is a photo of Terry with the Modernaires, one of our élite singing groups,' she said.

So D'Arby *did* start his music career in school! There he was in the group photo, third from the right, his thin wrists dangling from the sleeves of a rented tuxedo. The caption read: 'The DHS Modernaires is a working family of 16 singers and four accompanists under the direction of Mr David Martin. Membership in the Modernaires presents a year of fun, new friends, travel, endless smiling, stepping on your partners' toes and countless hours of hard work. Each member of the Modernaires is devoted to creating the finest performing group possible, because standing ovations, invitations to sing across the country, and superior ratings at State Contest come only with the dedication and determination the Modernaires display.'

'Let's see,' the secretary continued, 'there should also be one of him in the picture for the Senior Musical . . . and of course for Mr DHS . . . '

Mr DHS?

The secretary explained that every year there's a contest to choose the most popular and talented boy in DeLand High School. Terry Darby was one of the finalists in this 'Mr DHS' competition.

What!? Terence Trent D'Arby, the disaffected pop star who had told me he wanted to show up at his high school reunion and shove his success in everybody's face, was, in fact, nearly voted 'Most Popular' by his classmates? This was all too much. But there it was, in black and white, in the back of the **Athenian**, listed in an impressive resumé of D'Arby's high school activities: 'Mr DHS Finalist'. If D'Arby had been an alienated 'bad boy', he'd done a good job of fooling everyone at DeLand High. This looked like the career of a successful college-bound student. He had even belonged to the Football club and the Drama club.

'Terence Trent Darby, 3/15/62: Student Council Rep. 10; Football Mgr. 10; Adv. Chorus 10–11–12; Modernaires 12; Mr. DHS Finalist; Drama Club 10–12; "Odd Couple" 12; "Carnival" 12.'

The school secretary turned to

TTD

another section of the book, to D'Arby's formal graduation portrait. 'As you can see,' she observed, 'he was a scrawny kid, small for his age. And maybe that's why he has bad feelings about high school. But gosh, it was only a couple of months ago that he talked to the people at the **Sun News** and spoke so highly of his teachers here. He mentioned a few of them by name – Stan Whitted, and Mildred Clarke – and gave them all the credit for his success. You should really go over and talk to the people at the newspaper. They can tell you everything.'

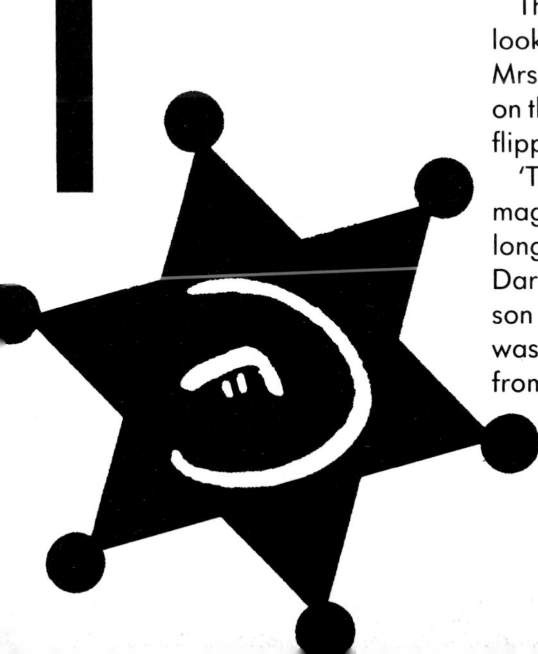

In five minutes, I was at the offices of the **DeLand Sun News**.

'You have to play me your interview tape. I can't believe Terry said that stuff about DeLand.' Karen Kirkpatrick, the **Sun News** staff reporter covering the 'Darby beat', led me out of the front newsroom into her boss's empty office, closed the door, and we sat down to talk. Kirkpatrick, a friendly, attractive woman with long ash-blonde hair, had been on the Darby story for months, ever since his mother Frances wandered into the newspaper office with a pile of her son's European press material.

'It was sometime in the beginning of last summer,' Kirkpatrick recalled. 'I happened to walk into the outer office, and there was a woman handing a bunch of press clippings to the secretary at the front desk, saying something about her son. We have people coming in here all the time trying to get themselves in the paper, so our secretary wasn't paying much attention to the lady. When I passed by, the secretary introduced the lady to me, figuring I'd handle things.'

Then, Kirkpatrick recounted, she looked at the press material that Mrs Frances Darby was pushing on the secretary. And she nearly flipped.

'These were top European magazines. Rave reviews, and long features. Everything Mrs Darby was saying was true; her son was becoming a star.' And it was all happening to somebody from DeLand, Florida.

Kirkpatrick took Mrs Darby's clips, and kept in touch. Mrs Darby continued to send more information. Soon, Kirkpatrick had amassed a large file on Terence Trent D'Arby. The folder, which she brought out to show me, was even larger than the package I'd received from CBS.

Then, in May 1987, just before D'Arby was ready to release his album in England, Frances Darby called Karen Kirkpatrick. Did she want to interview her son?

D'Arby called from London that evening. 'He was very sweet, and so excited about what was happening,' Kirkpatrick said. 'He asked me all about DeLand, and told me that if he won the Grammy, he'd send it to one of his music teachers at DeLand High, Mrs Mildred Clarke. What was really funny is that about five minutes after we hung up, he called me back. "Karen," he said, "I forgot to tell you . . . I've been nominated for a British Grammy for newcomer of the year . . . " '

Kirkpatrick's first stories on Terence Trent D'Arby ran in the May 16–17, 1987 edition of the **DeLand Sun News**. She searched through her folder and gave me a copy. The front-page headline proclaims: DHS Grad Plays at Montreux; credits DeLand Teachers. The article opens with a quote from a local radio DJ, who affirms that the Montreux Pop Festival is 'quite a deal.' Then it goes on to spring the news that a 'DeLand man' is one of the festival's closing acts. D'Arby is quoted as saying he loves his

If you all get to heaven Say a prayer for my mother Say a prayer for my father . . . Say a prayer for us all.

parents very much, and that Mrs Mildred Clarke was the person most responsible for him making the transition from singing gospel to singing popular music. D'Arby says he'd like to see Mrs Clarke again, to be able to tell her that all her work was not in vain.

Kirkpatrick then interviewed Mrs Clarke, who had been a music teacher at the junior high school until her retirement the previous year. Kirkpatrick had to inform Mrs Clarke about her former student's amazing success – she hadn't heard about it. But she is effusive in her praise for Terry Darby. 'He always had so much talent,' she says. 'I started him in music in the seventh grade . . . I recognized his talent when he was in my class.' (note: a seventh grader is about 12 years old.)

Clarke then describes how she would stay after school with Darby in her own time, trying to teach him how to read music. 'Terry not only sang well, he played drums well. He was very versatile.'

Terry Darby had been the soloist in her singing group, 'Sounds of the Seventies'. 'Everywhere we appeared,' she recounts, 'when Terry sang solo, he almost always got a standing ovation.' She concludes by telling the story of how one day Darby came to her and said that he wanted to get into sports. 'I told him it was a nice thing to get involved in, but not to give up music.'

It was a sweet, heartwarming

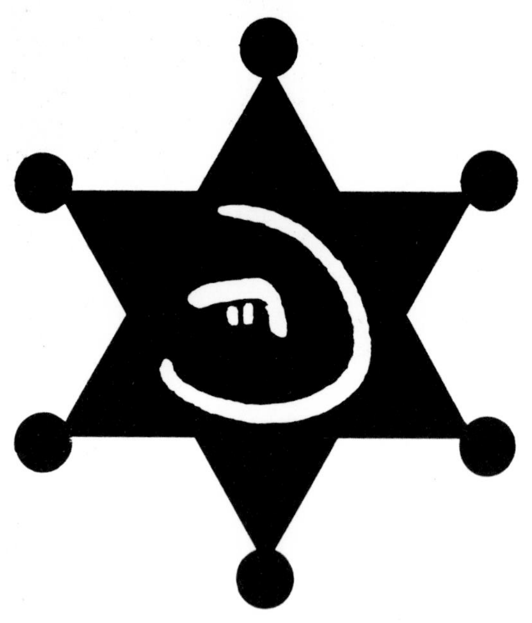

article. By way of contrast, I played Karen Kirkpatrick some of the choicer moments of *my* interview with Terence Trent D'Arby.

'Wow,' she laughed, 'this doesn't even sound like the same person I talked to. He must be going through something.'

She suggested that maybe D'Arby was trying to be more 'cool' with the New York press than he was with the folks back home. Or, perhaps, he was trying to play games, and create an image that fitted better with rock and roll stardom. I told her that D'Arby had almost had me believing that he was a high school delinquent troublemaker who'd run away first from home, and then from the army. And that I'd half-expected to come to DeLand and find out he'd been a drug dealer, or leader of a gang. Kirkpatrick laughed again.

'No way. His mother wouldn't have any of that in her house. All her children are good kids; hard workers, involved in school sports, in the community, in their dad's church. But you should talk to Frances while you're down here, she could tell you a lot more.'

Do you think she'd mind talking to me?

'Mind? She loves to talk about her son. The Darbys live really close by. Why don't you give Frances a call?'

She gave me the number. I called, and asked to speak to Frances Darby.

'She's not in right now.' A male voice. 'May I ask who's calling?'

I explained who I was, and that I wanted to interview Terence Trent D'Arby's mother.

'Well – harrumph! – and wouldn't you like to interview his *father*, too?'

The Reverend James Benjamin Darby laughed, and invited me to come on over to the house.

I had a few hours before my appointment with the Darbys, so Karen Kirkpatrick and her friend, fellow **Sun News** reporter Nancy Stinson, took me on a tour of DeLand. As we drove around the Stetson University campus, they entertained me with town gossip, like the story of the circus dwarf who'd hung himself in what the coroner had declared an 'auto-erotic suicide'.

DeLand was by no means a typical American small town, they explained; it was full of oddball, offbeat characters. The combination of the lovely semi-rural setting, and the university environment, attracted artists and writers and other creative types with a yen to get away from it all. The flautist who was James Galway's mentor lived here; so did the ex-bass player from the sixties blues band Moby Grape (he was affiliated to the university, and designed high-tech new-age sound systems). And, to top it all off, the neighbouring village, Cassadaga, was populated entirely by psychic mediums of the Spiritualist church, who, for a small fee, would put you in touch with your dear departed relatives.

I asked the reporters what the racial situation was like in the town. They told me that they could only give me a white person's perspective on that question, but that relations seemed cordial. Blacks took an active role in DeLand's civic activities, and they were well-represented among the faculty and administration of the schools. Stinson observed that many of DeLand's most successful sons and daughters had come out of its black community. The Darbys weren't the only tight-knit, achievement-oriented family in town. In fact, the boy who'd edged out Terry Darby for the 'Mr DHS' title back in 1979 was also black. André Glover, now a professional opera singer in New York, was at

least as famous a DeLand success story as Terry Darby. (Darby and Glover may have been rivals, but that hadn't stopped D'Arby from acting as best man at Glover's wedding a few months before.)

We turned a corner, crossed an invisible line, entered DeLand's black neighbourhood. Kirkpatrick pointed out 'the projects' – Oakland Terrace Housing, where the Darbys had lived when Terry was in high school. It was a complex of tidy garden apartments, each with its own yard, similar to one of the smaller-town council estates in the UK. 'But the Darbys live in a different place now, in their own house in a development called Candlewood Oaks,' said Kirkpatrick. Like Oakland Terrace, Candlewood Oaks was predominantly black.

The street suddenly turned into a rural road; we'd left the centre of town. Stinson slowed at an intersection where there were about 15 black teenagers hanging about in front of a grocery/general store, flirting, joking, listening to tapes. To Terence Trent D'Arby? No, it was Michael Jackson's 'Beat It'.

Stinson told me that she used to travel out this way quite often, because in addition to her work for the **Sun News**, she's a musician and music teacher. One of DeLand's black Pentecostal churches – and there are quite a few along this road – hired her to play the piano at their service. She described it as a fantastic job: 'You wouldn't believe the singing talent there was in just that one church!' And there were plenty of churches like it in DeLand. It was no wonder the local school musical groups were always winning awards.

She pointed out the church she used to play for – a big grey warehouse-type structure that didn't look like a church at all. Across the road was another big grey building – another church?

Stinson laughed. 'That's a local juke joint. (note: a juke joint is a dance hall/club.) Sometimes during our service the music would be coming from there so loudly that the pastor of the church would have to leave in the middle of preaching, go over there, and tell them to settle down. They always did.'

So this had been Terence Trent D'Arby's world. Music, church, school activities, family, working hard, trying to live up to your parents', the community's – not to mention the Lord's – expectations. The land of record companies, publicists, charts and rock and roll hype seemed a long way from the back roads of DeLand, Florida. I tried to imagine young Terry Darby struggling with the structures of this community, trying to be a 'good boy'. All the while, yearning for something beyond what DeLand could offer. But what? He couldn't have had much of an idea, back then. It was also pretty certain that his hopes and dreams made him feel guilty and conflicted. The world around him drew very clear lines between right and wrong. You either spent Saturday night in the church, or in the juke joint. And even if you chose the juke joint, you still jumped to attention when the preacher came round.

I was beginning to understand why D'Arby had become so agitated when I brought up the subject of his past in our interview. The people in DeLand, and the teachers at DeLand High School, remembered Terry Darby, the shy, sweet, slight and studious choirboy who was the preacher's son. But that had been D'Arby's public face; inside was a hidden bomb of ego, anger, restlessness and

frustration just waiting to explode. And that's what *D'Arby* remembered.

As we continued to drive through the neighbourhoods of D'Arby's past, I thought back to my own experiences in the morally unambiguous world of Pentecostal Christianity. Ten years ago, I'd been among the believers, travelling on assignment through the heart of the American Bible Belt, in Oklahoma (the only state where there are more churches, per capita, than saloons!). I'd been on the trail of an up-and-coming Pentecostal preacher whose television services had caught my attention on late night TV, and who would make an interesting subject for a magazine profile. For a week I travelled with his entourage, and attended several services, or 'camp meetings' every day. In meeting after meeting I observed very ordinary people doing extremely extraordinary things, from falling into trance states in public, to collapsing in shivers, to donating half their life's savings to the ministry, all in the name of Our Lord Jesus Christ. It was impossible to walk away from those services without being moved by the strong, genuine faith of the congregations; nevertheless I came home from the Bible belt upset and depressed. Something about it didn't feel right. I never wrote that magazine article, but years later, I would wish I had: the name of the preacher was Jimmy Swaggart.

Swaggart was a fiery minister, and an extremely successful one, even back then. He was also a fine musician, who'd learned to play hot rock and roll piano from the same teacher as his cousin, Jerry Lee Lewis. Swaggart used that family connection to advantage in his preaching, portraying himself as the 'good guy' who, after much struggle with worldly temptation, found happiness with the Lord. Jerry Lee Lewis, on the other hand, was the fallen angel, who'd sold his soul to the devil for cheap rock and roll thrills.

Swaggart's life story is a classic illustration of the psychological conflicts experienced by fundamentalist Christians. When he was a young boy, his parents were converted to the Pentecostal faith. (This was not an unusual happening in that day and age; after the first World War, the American South was full of itinerant preachers, black and white, who travelled from town to town spreading the gospel among poor farm and working people.) To be 'converted' meant the same thing as it does in the Pentecostal faith today; you must have a direct, personal confrontation with the Lord. This experience is intense, and can come in many different forms, but usually manifests itself physically. The Holy Spirit 'comes down', the way it did on the heads of Jesus's apostles in the Bible during Pentecost (where the sect gets its name). Sometimes the Spirit makes you shake, cry, or roll on the floor in ecstasy. Another common manifestation is glossolalia, or 'speaking in tongues', in which you go into a semi-trance, and babble in an unknown language, praising the Lord. (Anthropologists who have taped and analysed this phenomenon theorize that 'tongue speaking' is linguistically related to ancient Sanskrit!)

Every Pentecostal meeting, whether it's a simple Sunday service, or a huge outdoor revival crowded with thousands of people, has one purpose: to help still more souls reach this personal and emotional catharsis of faith. The structure of these services, whether it is in a black or white church, is always the same. There is music, group prayer, singing. Sometimes a second-string preacher will get up to the pulpit and do a 'warm up', or perhaps some of the already-sanctified will be invited to give testimony in front of the congregation. Finally, the climax of the meeting comes with the gospel sermon of the main preacher. A successful preacher is not only a skilled orator, and a great showman, but a brilliant amateur psychologist. He (or she) knows when the crowd is ready to be taken another step closer to the edge, and will build up the tension until the congregation is worked up to a fever pitch. At the end of the sermon, when the preacher invites his congregation to come forward and 'be saved', all hell breaks loose (if the preacher has done a good job). Many people will be weeping, trembling and shaking. During the Swaggart crusades, I saw quite a few staid old ladies rolling around on the floor. I asked one of these women, after she recovered her composure, what she'd felt. 'The pure love of my saviour Jesus Christ was in me,' she'd answered blissfully. Her eyes said everything: she was on cloud nine. Whatever had happened to her had been powerful, and positive. The 'high' of this spiritual experience is one of the reasons why Pentecostal religion (and in this sense it is not any different from the Afro-Caribbean sects of voodoo and santeria) has been so popular in America since the beginning of the 19th century.

Swaggart's mother 'got the spirit' first, then his father and grandmother. Of course there was enormous pressure on young Jimmy to 'get it', too. He didn't, at first. But he'd go over to visit his grandmother, and urge her to do tongue-speaking. (Once converted, a believer fills with the Holy Spirit, and things like glossolalia happen as routinely as hiccuping.) After a while, young Jimmy gave up doing 'sinful' things like going to the movies on Saturday (with his devilish cousin!). Then, one day in church, it happened. He heard the Lord whispering in his ear. And, before you knew it, Swaggart had the 'gift of tongues', too. His mother was overjoyed.

The life of a believer, however, is not an easy road. The devil, the Pentecostals warn, is hiding in every corner, disguised in the form of the everyday world and its temptations. By the time he was a teenager, Swaggart's attention turned away from the church. He

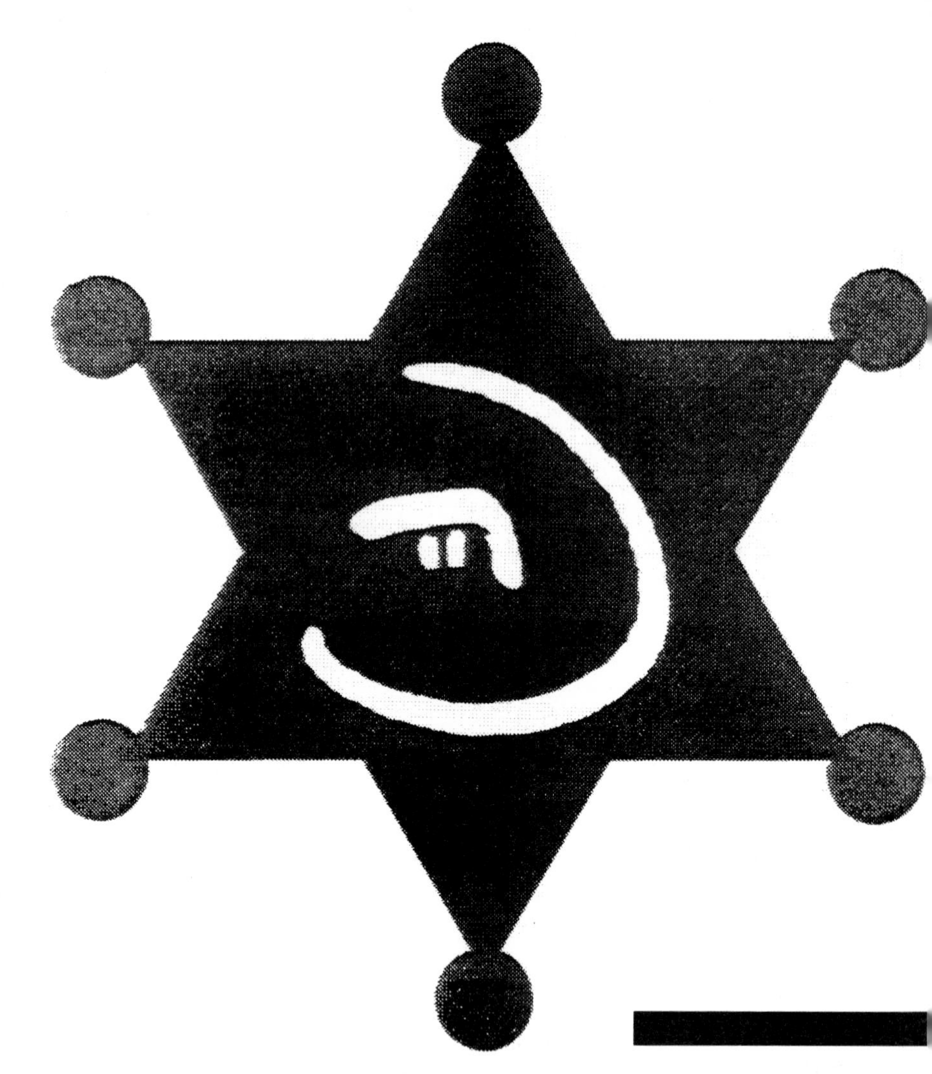

D'Arby's mother with his music teacher Mrs Clarke, holding the Grammy Award.

spent his time chasing girls and hanging out with Jerry Lee. His parents prayed for him and – at least this is the way Swaggart recounted it ten years ago – their prayers were answered. Swaggart 'came home' to Jesus Christ, and commenced his career as a preacher. But the battle between the devil and the Lord for possession of Swaggart's soul wasn't over. 30 years or so later, in a prostitute's motel room in Baton Rouge, Louisiana, the devil had his day.

Swaggart's conversion, fall from grace, and subsequent remorse is not an unusual story in the annals of fundamentalist religion. Quite the contrary; Swaggart's tale is almost an American cliché. America, especially these days, is overpopulated with sinners-turned saints-turned sinners. It's a nation that just loves to repent. Preachers like Swaggart and Jim and Tammy Faye Bakker are obvious examples, but politicians also get in on the act (Charles Coulson, Watergate convict, was 'born again' in prison, and now preaches. Former President Jimmy Carter created a small scandal when he told an interviewer that he 'lusted in his heart'). Then there are the musicians: Jerry Lee Lewis has had several relationships with the church. So has Little Richard, who used to be a Pentecostal preacher, then publicly declared his homosexuality from the pulpit, then converted to Judaism. Marvin Gaye, or so says his biographer, had incredible conflicts with his sexuality which can be traced to his relationship with his father, a preacher, and his church background. Al Green fell away from his gospel roots, became a soul singing legend, and a notorious ladies' man; then he got hit with a bowl of hot grits thrown by a jealous ex-lover. Now he's the Reverend Al Green, singing only gospel music.

Why are there so many musicians associated with fundamentalism? Probably because music is so fundamental to the church. Singing, like glossolalia, is considered to be a gift of the holy spirit, an expression of Gold's power and love. In Pentecostal churches, especially black ones, this belief in the power of the spirit enables singers to reach vocal peaks that would be impossible otherwise. (I know two professional singers who've struggled with the issue of whether to sing pop music, or to stay strictly gospel. They always go back to the church. As one explained, 'It's never as good outside.')

For a Pentecostal, the conflict never ends. You fall away from the church in order to come back stronger in the faith, in order to have your faith put to the test again. There is no compromise, no middle ground; one is saved, or one is damned. There's no room to be human. 'Too often the life they convince you they want you to lead – the life they *tell* you to lead – isn't a human life at all. It's a super human life,' D'Arby had commented in our interview. D'Arby said he became disillusioned with the church because of the hypocrisy he observed among the people who were supposedly following its beliefs. Obviously, D'Arby no longer counted himself among the believers – or did he? The power of the Pentecostal faith is strong, and not easily cast aside, especially for someone brought up in the church. Had D'Arby really been able to shake the Pentecostal world-view out of his system, or did he still believe, somewhere deep inside, that God and the devil were locked in a wrestling match for his soul? Maybe that was something that his father, the Reverend Darby, would be able to tell me.

Karen Kirkpatrick took me to the Darbys'. During the trip, she told me more about the family. Besides Reverend and Mrs Darby, there were five children still living at home. Sherry, at 21, was the oldest; she was a student at nearby Daytona Beach Community College. Lisa, 18, was also enrolled at Daytona Beach College. 15-year-old Darren, the next-oldest brother, attended DeLand High, and made local headlines even more often than his famous brother, because he was a star of the school football team. There were two smaller boys: André, aged 12, and Davian, aged

5. In addition, Mrs Darby's sister, Barbara Howard, had lived with the family for the past 17 years. The Reverend Darby had moved his family to Daytona Beach in 1973, and settled in DeLand the following year. Currently, he was pastor of DeLand's Refuge Church of Our Lord Jesus Christ, and he also served as chairman of the international board of evangelists of that Pentecostal denomination. Both Darbys, Kirkpatrick informed me, were well-educated; the Reverend had a bachelor's degree in Psychology from Central Florida University in Orlando, and Mrs Darby was a few credits short of her master's degree in Psychological Counselling.

We parked in front of a small brown concrete bungalow in an estate of similar houses called 'Candlewood Oaks' (there were no oaks in sight), and walked up to the door. A familiar smile greeted us and invited us inside: Sherry.

The aroma of cooking food filled the house. Darby brothers wandered casually in and out of the parlour. We sat down in a cosy sitting room filled with pictures and memorabilia. On the coffee table sat an ornamental plaque that read 'To Pastor and Wife', and there were numerous sports trophies proudly displayed on a cabinet. The eye was drawn to a wall of framed photographs over the sofa: acid-bright Kodachromes of family members, a crumbling shot of a young couple on the streets of a Northern city, and, in the middle of the arrangement, a faded sepia-toned print of a handsome woman with pale skin, high cheekbones, and huge, dreamy hazel eyes. Her eyes seemed to be looking toward the opposite wall, which was also covered, but not with photographs. This wall was hung with the trophies of rock stardom: gold and platinum records that all said: 'Terence Trent D'Arby'.

'That was my mother,' said Frances Darby, when she saw me looking at the woman's portrait. 'Terry always looked like her . . . the light skin, the hazel eyes . . .'

Mrs Darby sat down on the sofa. Then Reverend Darby entered the parlour. He was dressed formally, in a three-piece pinstriped suit, and he had a gentle, but dignified demeanour, one that instantly commanded respect. I could easily imagine him in the pulpit before a congregation.

They Darbys listened as I introduced myself, and explained what I was doing. They didn't seem surprised I had come, even though they told me they hadn't done any interviews, except with Karen Kirkpatrick, and another local reporter. They would be glad, they said, to talk to me about their son; he was in close touch with the family, and they were very proud of him.

I decided not to mention anything about the negative things their son had told me in connection with DeLand; nor could I bring myself to ask them about his moody, combative behaviour. The Reverend and Mrs Darby impressed me as trusting, good people who were full of love for their son. I wondered, however, whether they had read all, or any of D'Arby's brash, controversial British interviews. Had they seen the promotional photo of their son, dressed and posed as Jesus Christ on the cross, in the **News of the World**?

Mrs Darby, a cheerful, plump woman whose face was a darker, rounder version of her son's, began by answering my question about D'Arby and singing:

(Mrs Darby) Yes, Terence has been singing since he was small. Terry started out when he was younger with his sisters, singing together in the church. That's where he got his training as far as singing is concerned. But my husband could tell you better.

Reverend Darby cleared his throat, and looked at me thoughtfully. He seemed to be pleased that his wife deferred the conversation to him.

Terry was the one into music. The other boys went more into sports. Terry was a bit philosophical. He was always a little different from the norm. Like the arts. From the time he was young he could sit down and tell you things about the arts. If you sit and talk with him you could see pieces of that coming out in his writing. Not his music, but in his other writing. Like he wrote one article for the **DeLand Sun News**, an article about stray dogs. He was training for boxing and he used to jog, but he was always getting chased by dogs. So he wrote an article decrying against dogs running loose.

Sometimes Terry's moody. Sometimes he lets it all hang out.

I asked the Reverend how old his son was when he started to sing.

Probably when he was about six or seven. Around the same age as his brother André was, of course André was more into sports, an all-rounder. André excelled at sports. Terry was into boxing. Terry started boxing when he was still in high school. I think he was 15 or 16. He was at the Sports Stadium in Orlando, and then he moved to the Church Street Gym.

Mrs Darby looked as though she had some definite views on this subject. I asked her if she liked the idea of her son becoming a boxer.

No I did *not*. I suppose I'm sort of a boxing fan, it depends on who's boxing. But when it comes to your eldest child, that's another thing altogether. Well, there wasn't much I could do, it was what he wanted to do.

(Rev Darby) I encouraged him to protect himself. Not to provoke fights, but to protect himself. Terry was always so small of build. And I suppose that's why he went into boxing. He went to karate school too to learn the martial arts. When I see him jump the way he does on stage, I think he probably got that from karate school.

I asked Reverend Darby to tell me a bit about himself, and what he's done in his life. For instance, I'd heard that he was once a professional baseball player. He warmed to the subject.

(Rev Darby) I've always been an athlete. I'm originally from Florida, and Frances' roots are in Florida too, but she grew up in New York and New Jersey. We've been married nearly 30 years. We're hangin' in there.

I've been a preacher since I was a teenager. You see, the ministry is a calling, a divine calling, and it doesn't come because one chooses it as a vocation. It comes with a divine calling, and I had a divine calling.

Reverend Darby explained that now he is the chairman of the international board of evangelists of his church. His position requires him to travel all over the continental United States and out of the country. So he understands some of the pressures and problems his son faces when he's touring out on the road.

I take the opportunity to change the subject back to the family's music. I ask Mrs Darby if it's true that she used to be a famous gospel singer.

(Mrs Darby) Yes, I used to sing with a gospel group out of New York. I don't believe I was famous. We made some records, but I don't think I still have them . . .

At home we still do sing as a family. Mostly it's the girls who sing, and André sings with a group in town that is supposed to be making a record. I direct the church choir with my sister and daughters. The congregation of the church is between 75 and 100 people.

(Rev Darby, interrupting) Can you hear me? I know I don't talk too loud. I've suffered since high school because of it. I have a

monotone.

Then, how can you be a preacher?
(Rev Darby, laughing) I'm lazy. I'm outspoken, but I'm lazy.

I ask him to tell me a bit about his expanding congregation, and his work as a minister.
(Rev Darby) In my church, I'm the main man. We have services at 11.30 on Sundays. It's a downright Pentecostal service. I guess my biggest success is my capacity as an evangelist. Bringing people to the Lord.

Reverend Darby says he's not one to boast, but that many people have commented on the power of his preaching. For example, one of his professors at Central Florida University, who is Jewish, came to see him preach one Sunday.
(Rev Darby) Well, I preached that morning, and I noticed he was there, but he left before the end of the service. Later he told me, 'Reverend Darby, I just had to get my behind out of there!' Later on, he was giving a lecture in his class and he said, 'I was in Reverend Darby's church last Sunday. He had my wife, and he almost got me!'

What about Terry? Did he rebel against your strong beliefs, or against authority, when he was an adolescent?
(Rev Darby, thoughtfully) Terry wasn't openly rebelling. We never had any discipline problems with him, except . . . Well the way we solved that problem after Terry left home is that we let all the kids have their own music boxes and their own televisions in their rooms. But when Terry was growing up, it was strictly gospel. I do watch Terry on TV, though . . .

(At this moment, Lisa and André begin to giggle. Their mother shoots them a cross look.)
(Mrs Darby) No, we never had any problem, even, you know, how kids will want to go out and stay out too late. When Terry would go out, he'd just be going over to one of his teacher's houses, like Stan Whitted's.
(Rev Darby) His company was very good company. There were kids who were in the same interest groups as he was, school groups. We didn't even have to reinforce anything, it was voluntary. Terry did, however, have problems at times in school. It was out of frustration. Kids picked on him.
(Mrs Darby) Yes. Terry, because of his size and all was picked on. He was also a grade ahead of himself in school, he had skipped a grade, so he was a little younger than the kids in his grade, and that caused problems. Terry wanted to be accepted. He never really wanted to appear too smart. He never tried to excel. He wouldn't sit down and study, but he'd make the honor roll [*register*] just by going to school. He tried to be accepted by the other kids, but they just picked on him.

OPEN
POLICE
DEPT
NEW YORK
LIVE TO RIDE

DeLand Sun News

111th Year Weekend, May 16-17, 1987

DHS grad plays at Montreux; credits DeLand teachers

☐ RELATED STORY, SHOWCASE MAGAZINE

By KAREN KIRKPATRICK
Sun News/Enterprise Writer

It's the elite gathering of the greats in the popular music world. By invitation only. "It's quite a deal, it really is," said Mick Dolan, promotional director of WDIZ radio. It's the Montreux Pop Festival in Switzerland, and it's taking place right now.

The interesting angle here is that a DeLand man is one of the festival's closing acts.

D'Arby at 19

Terence Trent D'Arby, 25, better known to local folk as Terry Darby, DeLand High School Class of 1979, will be presented with the "Newcomer of the Year Award" from the British equivalent of MTV, Music Box.

"I'm the last act before Whitney Houston," D'Arby told the Sun News from London Wednesday. He was scheduled to leave Thursday for the festival.

The festival is so highly regarded throughout the world, Dolan said, that just to attend as a spectator is "a once-in-a-lifetime experience."

When his first hit record and pre-released cuts from his new albums began circulating in England within the last two to three months, D'Arby was immediately called the new singing sensation of Great Britain by the British press.

His first single has been No. 7 on the pop charts for three weeks. He has released a video (which has already shown up on MTV here), and people over there are buying up D'Arby T-shirts and posters.

In a telephone interview from London Wednesday, D'Arby said that other than his parents, the Rev. James and Florence Darby of DeLand whom he "loves very much," "Mrs. Mildred Clark was probably the person most responsible for helping me make the transition" from singing strictly gospel to popular music. "I owe a great, great debt to her," D'Arby said. "When I win my Grammy I'm going to send it to her." He also said he "would just love to see her" in order to prove all her work with him was not in vain.

Clark was a music teacher at DeLand Junior High School until her retirement last year. When told of D'Arby's success in Europe, Clark spared no words in her praise for him. "He always had so much talent. I started him in music in the seventh grade.... I recognized his talent when he was in my class."

Clark said she used to stay after school with D'Arby "on my own time" to teach him how to read music. "He was my soloist in the 'Sounds of the 70s,'" she said, adding that "Terry not only sang well, he played drums well. He was very versatile.

"Everywhere we appeared, when Terry sang solo he almost always got a standing ovation." Clark said that as a trained professional, she "could recognize God-given talent. You have to have the innate talent first before it can be developed."

She said, "He came to me one day; he wanted to get into sports. I told him it was a nice thing to get involved in, but not to give up music," she remembers.

D'Arby was the regional Golden Gloves lightweight champion of Florida in 1979.

D'Arby mentioned two other DeLand teachers who have helped and influenced him in his musical career: David Martin, the choral director at DeLand High School; and Stan Whitted, an administrative assistant at DHS, former history teacher and

Please see DHS GRAD, 2A

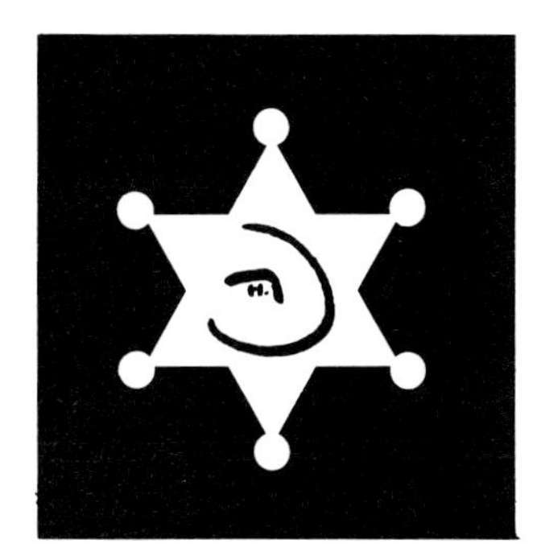

Did Terry's being black add to his trouble? Was there a problem with him being a minority in a white school? Or not being accepted among blacks because of his white skin?
(Mrs Darby) Not in the family. Terry's always been the favourite in the family. Well, he's not the only light-skinned person in the family. I have nieces and nephews in the family who are light-skinned, and I have a cousin who is light-skinned. His grandmother was really light-skinned. Maybe at school this gave Terry problems, but in the family, no. To be honest with you, Terry was quite spoiled. On both sides of the family, he was spoiled.
(Rev Darby) Terry always received attention. And he had to be the centre of attention. He loved attention, and at home he got it. But at school he didn't get that special attention all of the time. I'm not saying I have the exact answer, but I think that's what caused his frustration at school . . .

One of his music teachers at school, Mrs Mildred Clark, she was the person who convinced me to allow Terry to sing something besides gospel. She said to me, 'You know, your son could make you a millionaire.'

I always let him make his own decisions. When he was 17, he wanted to go in the Army and I wouldn't sign for him. I said, you have to wait till you're 18. I didn't want him turning around and saying to me, 'Daddy, you shouldn't have done that.'
(Mrs Darby) I think his choice of the Army had to do with the boxing. The recruiting officer misdirected him, and led him to think that joining the Army was a great opportunity to box. But then he found out that to get to Fort Bragg, which had the big Army boxing school, he would've had to sign up to be a paratrooper, and he told me, 'Mom, I don't want to jump out of airplanes.'
(Rev Darby) I just think he lost the will to box.
(Mrs Darby) Which I was glad for.
(Rev Darby) And it's funny how things work out. He was in Oklahoma, at Fort Sill, when he started working on his music again. He met Billy Preston at a concert and gave him a tape.
(Mrs Darby) I think that was really when he started taking his music seriously. You know he taught himself to play keyboard. He played drums from when he was five years old. He tells me now how he wishes he learned how to read music in high school.

Why do you think he's so unwilling to talk about all this with the press?
(Rev Darby) I think he wants to be a little mysterious. In my ministry, I like to be a little mysterious, too.

He went on to tell me how Terry calls home at least once a week. Often, it's to ask his advice on artistic matters like what song he should sing at the forthcoming Grammy awards. The Reverend explained that the whole family is going up to New York to see Terry when he appears on the Grammys. He, of course, will be at the hotel, not at the actual ceremony. You see, he doesn't approve of that sort of thing.
(Rev Darby) I'm not an advocate of pop music. Terry understands that. His career puts the family in a difficult situation because . . . Basically, I preach against all that stuff.

Terry's doing what he wants to

The *DeLand Sun News* celebrates the town's rising star. *Inset*: D'Arby (encircled) singing in a youth choir (from *In Fashion* magazine, September 1988).

do, what makes him happy, and he's living a positive life. Even though it isn't what I would want for him. I respect him, and he respects me. You know, I sang pop music when I was coming up. I had my guitar, put on my big pants, and imitated Elvis Presley and Little Richard. I loved baseball as a boy, too. I was real good. But when the time came, I made the change.

His face appeared grave: a man of powerful, deeply held moral convictions, trying to reconcile them with his love and pride for his son, who breaks most of his rules. How does he do it?

When I asked him that question, he and Mrs Darby broke into smiles.

(Rev Darby) There's something that we know, but we don't think it's time to expose it yet. There are some roads we don't choose ourselves, but that are chosen for us. I don't think money is Terry's goal. Attention is. I think he's gonna do this for a while, and then . . .

Suddenly, the phone rang – it was KP's office in New York, calling to check on arrangements for the Grammy trip. Reverend Darby went into the kitchen to speak to KP's assistant. I heard him say that he was in the middle of chatting with a reporter.

He came back into the parlour, and we continued our chat. But not for long: less than five minutes after the first call, the phone rang again. It was Terry, from London.

Reverend Darby went back into the kitchen to take the call. When he returned, he was visibly embarrassed and upset.

'My son wants me to tell you . . . uh . . . that he isn't pleased you came here,' he said hesitantly.

I was upset too. The Darbys were good people, and through them I'd started to gain a deeper understanding of the difficult, moody rock singer I'd encountered – it seemed like months, not weeks ago. Thanks to the family, and DeLand, I'd been able to put together a picture of the bright, shy, ambitious and confused 'favourite son' in place of the over-hyped, combative pop star. I was beginning to like Terry Darby, but I wasn't so sure about Terence Trent Apostrophe.

I thanked Reverend and Mrs Darby for their time and kindness, and asked the Reverend if *he* was displeased I came to see them, and he said no. I told him I didn't understand why his son was so unwilling to let people know who he really was, and what he came from.

The Reverend shook his head slowly, and for an instant his face appeared to bear the burdens of the world. 'He loves the attention, but the work is taking its toll. He calls me and says, "Dad, I'm so tired." '

As we stood up to say goodbye, the Reverend recovered his composure. 'This is just a temporary thing. He's not gonna be there forever.'

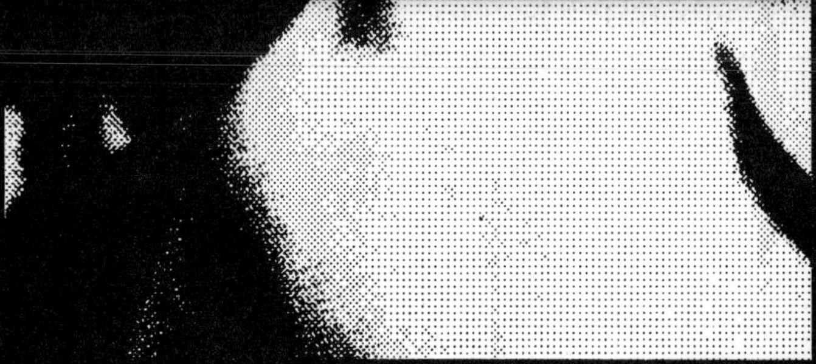

Portrait

5.

chapter

s

of the

Artist

Portraits of the Artist

Frances Darby lent me two snapshots of her son. The first had been taken when he was about 19 years old, in an Army training camp in Oklahoma. He wears a t-shirt that says: 'Brown Fox Golden Gloves', and he's looking mean. In just a few years, the scrawny boy of the yearbook photo has turned into a man; the muscles in his arms are hard, and he appears about ten pounds heavier than he does in recent shots. There's nothing androgynous about this D'Arby.

The other picture almost seemed to be of a different person. It had been taken at home in DeLand, sometime after D'Arby got out of the Army. He must have been around 21. This D'Arby is beginning to look like a rock and roll hero; he's thinner, his face is softer, and he's dressed in a loose, Hawaiian-style shirt. His hair is a Jimi Hendrix crown of black curls, and his earlobe is pierced with a gold ring.

Back in my hotel room that evening, I placed the pictures in a row: First, the gangly 'Mr DHS' finalist of the yearbook; then the muscled, athletic Army boxer, then the Hendrix hippie, and finally, the model-gorgeous publicity photo from the CBS press kit. The four faces of Terence Trent D'Arby. The pictures told a story of amazing change and self-transformation. How were they connected? Reverend and Mrs Darby had certainly been helpful in filling in some of the pieces, but they were, after all, D'Arby's parents. There were things they couldn't possibly know.

The following day, I tried to find someone to talk to who might have a different, more objective perspective on D'Arby. Stan Whitted, one of the teachers mentioned in Kirkpatrick's **Sun News** article, had taught Terry Darby in history class and worked closely with him as a vocal coach in a community singing group that he runs. As a teacher and friend, and as a black role model in a predominantly white school and town, I thought that Whitted would have a special insight into the personality and talents of his former student. And certainly he'd be able to tell me if D'Arby's bitterness about the US had anything to do with racism he'd experienced in DeLand.

Whitted was now an assistant principal at the junior high school in nearby Deltona, Florida. But it

was Saturday, and school was closed. I reached him at home, over the phone. Whitted, as I'd suspected, had many thoughtful things to say about his famous ex-student.

(Stan Whitted) Terry was in my group of community singers called the Cantileers. We were a highly disciplined group that rehearsed twice a week and we sang at community functions and banquets around DeLand. At the time Terry was in the group, there were about 30 members between the ages of 13 and 17. We sang contemporary gospel music, like Walter Hawkins and James Cleveland, and some popular tunes.

Did you think that Terry would go on to do something in music?

Not at that time. It was a very competitive group. Terry was very good, but there were better singers in it. Terry always had multiple interests, not just singing. He was always looking or searching for something. He is a brilliant person with a high degree of interpretive ability. But back in high school he was very introverted, and very shy.

Did Terry's shyness have anything to do with his being black in a predominantly white community?

I don't think it was being black in a predominantly white high school that affected him so much as the fact that he had to compete as a singer with four other young men who were as good as, if not better than, he was. And they had more outgoing personalities, and got more recognition in the community. That really got to Terry. We had a lot of talent in that year. Any one of those boys I worked with could have become the superstar. One of the other boys in the Cantileers, André Glover, has been in several jazz ensembles, toured Europe, and now sings opera professionally.

From a technical, professional level, how would you rate the singing on his first LP?

At times there is a lack of vocal training that shows in him. I think that's because of his religious background, and his singing in his father's church. Much of the church singing is done acapella, and you don't learn to focus on the pitch of an instrument. Although Terry had been in a lot of school groups that were also very competitive, like the Sounds of the Seventies and the Modernaires, he never developed that sense of vocal placement. Yes, there are times on his album when he is out of key.

The part of Terry's voice that is really the Terry I remember is that middle range of his, which has a Sam Cooke-Stevie Wonder quality. You hear it in the beginning of 'Wishing Well'. That's the Terry I know. I also remember when Terry was running for Mr DHS, he sang this Commodores song, 'Three Times A Lady', and I heard for the first time this really vibrant, alive tone. Terry didn't have his own style. His ability to sound like so many other artists was his way then. And it is his way now. If he'd gotten more training, he'd be an even better singer.

Was he a discipline problem in high school?

Well, I would hate to contradict him, but Terry was always a well-mannered person. Terry was blessed with the ability to do many different things. How many kids can be a singer, a writer, and a Golden Gloves boxer? That's why he was confused. In class he was brilliant, with a high degree of interpretive ability, but only when he was motivated. Terry had the academic ability to be the smartest boy in DeLand High School if he had applied himself to that. But he was going off in several directions at once. If he was a rebel, then he was a very quiet rebel.

Whitted's observations confirmed the impressions of D'Arby I'd got from the DeLand High yearbook, and from the family. D'Arby had been a bright, multi-talented, shy and well-mannered boy who craved recognition. But Whitted's story added a new twist: D'Arby hadn't received the attention he wanted, at least not in music. According to his music teacher, D'Arby had been a good singer, but not the best. He'd been frustrated by this (another good reason for his anger about DeLand, years later). And so, he turned to other areas besides music to try and make his mark.

D'Arby had told me, and a few other English writers, that he'd been active on the school paper, and had worked as a journalist in Florida. But the DeLand High yearbook didn't list him as an editor at the school newspaper. And nobody at the **DeLand Sun News** could recall D'Arby having worked at the paper. Both D'Arby and his father had mentioned a particular article, the one about the dogs running loose in the street. Was this article ever printed? Weeks later, Karen Kirkpatrick discovered the answer: D'Arby hadn't written for the high school's newspaper (he'd been the editor of his junior high paper, at the age of 12), nor for the **Sun News**, but he *had* written a letter to the editor of the paper that had been published in 1979. This was the piece:

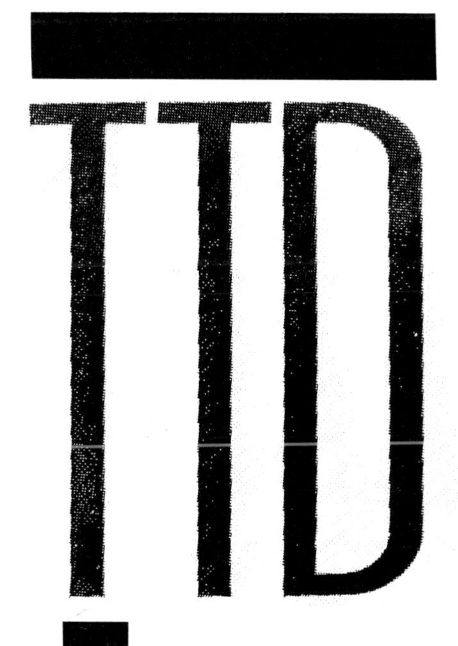

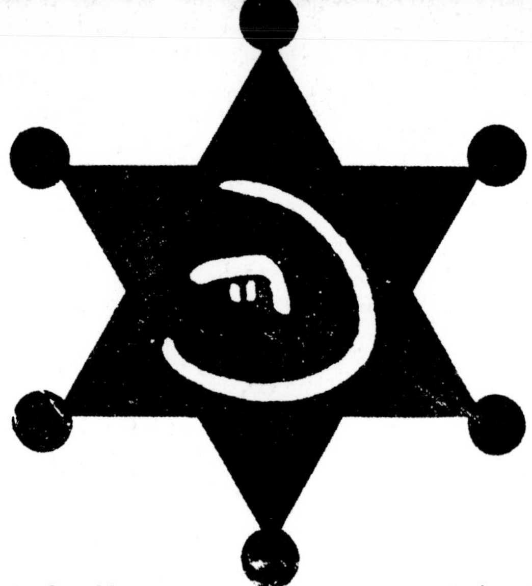

Editor, **Sun News**:

As a young citizen of DeLand, class of '79, and now of voting age, I have a complaint which I am daring you to publish in full. It concerns dog control.

I live in Oakland Terrace Housing area and, because I am a firm believer of physical fitness, if it weren't for my love of boxing, I wouldn't be running three miles in the darkness of night.

After being attacked and reattacked by seemingly wild dogs lap after lap, I am now questioning my dedication to my sport and the animal laws of the city.

No matter how domesticated dogs are supposed to be, it is still rather frightening to be chased to sanity's end by snarling and bite-hungry mutts.

Dog owners seem appalled at the idea that a runner would rap their precious pets on the head with an ancient means of protection, the stick, but not too sympathetic with the fact that their dogs seem to be making trophies out of runners' calves.

Where is the dogcatcher of comic lore? He always appears in the nick of time for Tom & Jerry. What has happened to the city ordinances concerning loose dogs and cats? (In defense of the cat, I prefer trying to outrun a feline.)

What really is unnerving is the sight of two grinning dog owners placing bets on whose dog snaps first.

I always thought dogs were domesticated to be used as pets, guardians of personal property or both. In the one-mile block that I run around, the pets are guarding the street. I find it quite annoying that during the few break-ins of cars or apartments, that dogs aren't a factor, in fact they seem to say to the wrongdoer, 'Oh, don't worry about me, I'm only into joggers.'

The laxity of city officials and police persons are to blame, along with pet owners. I have valid reason to believe that most owners around here haven't even seen to it that their dogs receive proper shots anyway, for sick and mangy animals abound around here.

The only benefit of being chased by a canine is once you're through with your mileage, you feel as though you've run twice the distance.

Although I have tried to remain calm and find humor in this uncontrollable situation, I am totally serious. I've been instructed by a legal mind that if bitten or even having taken a bad fall from the threat of an animal, the owner and the city of DeLand can be sued for negligence of the owner and failure to carry out a law or ordinance, respectively. (Lawyer, has there ever been a precedent of a person shooting dog in a city zone in self-defense?)

The question is posed unto you the official: 'Shouldn't I have the right to run in my own neighborhood in a city where I pay taxes without being harassed? Need I carry the law into my own hands?'

My threat is serious, either the city takes action against these estranged beasts or I will!

Thank you for the platform,

Terry T Darby
DeLand

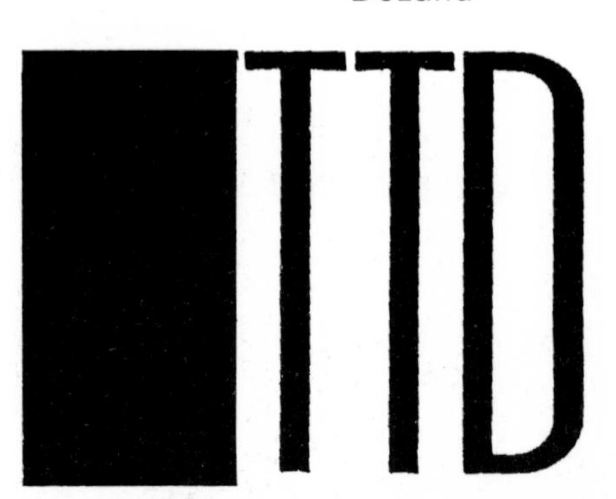

As Kirkpatrick read this letter to me over the phone, we were both convulsed with laughter over Darby's satiric, grandiloquent prose. Kirkpatrick observed that, even at the age of 18, Terry Darby was expressing himself with a slightly British inflexion ('It is still rather frightening . . .' 'I have valid reason to believe . . .'). I agreed, but thought that Darby's style smacked more of the Biblical rhetoric of the pulpit ('The question is posed unto you the official . . .'). Either way, one thing was evident: Terry Darby was precocious and talented, ambitious, and dying to be noticed. When he wrote that letter, his mind, and his dreams, were miles beyond the city limits of DeLand. Imagine the teenage Terry Darby of the letter running faster and further away from home, angry dogs nipping at the heels of his Adidas sneakers. What a metaphor for his frustrated adolescence!

He'd taken up boxing when he was 16, against his mother's wishes, and much to the dismay of his music teachers, who feared he was spreading himself too thin. D'Arby worked so hard that within two years he had achieved his first transformation: he was a contender. Once, then twice a week, he'd make the two-hour drive down to Orlando, to train at the Church Street Gym. It was his first step away from family and DeLand, and he made it count: in 1980, boxing as a lightweight, he won the Central Florida region's Golden Gloves championship.

Shortly thereafter, the US Army recruiter knocked on his door, with an alluring offer: the Army would send D'Arby away to the military's prestigious boxing school if he signed up. D'Arby wanted to join right away, but he was still a minor, and his father wouldn't sign the release form. 'I encouraged him to try college,' said Reverend Darby. D'Arby took his father's suggestion, and spent less than a year on a journalism scholarship at his father's alma mater, the University of Central Florida in Orlando. But he didn't like it, and dropped out. US Army records show that D'Arby entered the military service on 30 July, 1980 – exactly four and a half months after his 18th birthday on 15 March. (Which is a birthdate D'Arby shares, by bizarre coincidence, with Jimmy Swaggart!)

The US Army recruits Golden Gloves boxers as morale boosters. Each unit has its own contingent of champions who box as a team against teams from other units. The matches are usually held in recreation centres at the various posts, in front of hundreds, sometimes thousands of GIs. A champion boxer receives recognition and star treatment, and maybe this was the attraction that lured D'Arby into the Army. Or perhaps the idea of being a soldier appealed to his newfound self-image as a strong, physically mature male. (He'd mentioned in our interview that his mother had hoped the Army would make a 'man' out of her son. Then he'd laughed scornfully at what a ridiculous myth that was; but at the age of 18, perhaps he believed it, too.) Or maybe the Army simply represented the most convenient ticket out of DeLand. At any rate, as soon as he could, D'Arby jumped at the Army's offer.

Things didn't work out exactly the way he'd hoped. His mother's version of the story was that her son would have had to have gone to Fort Bragg and train as a paratrooper in order to go to boxing school; and Terry was afraid of jumping out of planes. The Reverend had said that his son 'lost the will to box'. D'Arby, in our interview, had told me that he became alienated and disillusioned with the military lifestyle almost as soon as he got in: 'I actually allowed people to brainwash me into thinking, "Yeah, Terence, maybe you *do* need to settle down into a groove and be a contributing, functioning member of a responsible community." All that sort of bollocks that you read about in Christmas cards and Norman Rockwell.' At any rate, he didn't get sent to boxing school, but was posted to Fort Sill, Oklahoma. There he was trained and classified as a 'unit supply specialist'. A supply clerk.

While in Fort Sill, D'Arby started to change tracks again, from boxing to music. As his mother and his sister Sherry had mentioned, he went up to keyboard player Billy Preston after a concert and handed him a homemade demo tape of his music, hoping that Preston might be able to help him.

But nothing came of it.

Then he was shipped overseas to join the Third Armored Division – Elvis Presley's old outfit – stationed near Frankfurt, West Germany. He'd never been outside the United States before, or so far away from home. The way D'Arby describes it, Germany was like a promised land: 'All of a sudden you stand in a spot and it starts to vibrate, you know? I felt like now I could be who I was without having to apologize.'

He also didn't have to compete with four other singers who were better than he was. In DeLand, D'Arby had been just another promising talent in a town full of gospel choirs. In Frankfurt, he was unique, a novelty.

'There is no German translation of the word "groove", and that tells you all,' Andrien Kreye explained to me, laughing. Kreye, a saxophonist, lived in Frankfurt and Munich in the early eighties, and used to play in the same club circuit as D'Arby. (He currently is an editor of the Germany magazine **Tempo**, and is based in New York.) Since he is both musician and writer, Kreye was able to give me a vivid description of the music scene in Germany at the time D'Arby arrived there.

'The popular style with the Munich session guys was jazz fusion. With some funk, some rock. And no rhythm. The more difficult chord changes you had, the better. Totally boring. But if the German bands could hire some black guys from the army, they began to sound better, and they would usually get more work.

'A black musician can really do well in a place like Germany. And it's a real ego trip. When D'Arby first came over, he immediately saw that there weren't too many black singers, and he must have figured, like, "Wow ... I'm the best over here."'

D'Arby had told me that he'd hung about in a music store in Frankfurt, chatted up some players, and landed himself a gig with a band called Touch. 'I hadn't sung in years, didn't even know if I could still hold a tune,' he'd explained. (This was not true: he'd been thinking about music seriously since handing the demo tape to Billy Preston the year before.) Anyway, he passed the audition and joined Touch. For the first time, Terence Trent D'Arby was in a band.

Andrien Kreye often saw Touch at Munich's Vilharmonie Club. 'They were pretty good, but Terry helped them a lot. This was around the time that Michael Jackson's **Thriller** came out, and Terry could sing in that style. People were calling him Germany's own Michael Jackson. He was the best. The best over here.'

The band's fortunes took off. So did D'Arby. He left his army base one night and didn't go back. 'I was in hiding,' is how he'd described that time in our interview. 'It was really romantic. Fugitive on the run. Serious rock and roll myth. Every gig, I wondered, would they catch me? Would this be my last gig for years?'

That's the Terence Trent D'Arby Legend. But the reality, as I discovered by speaking to military lawyers and specialists in Army procedure, is much less dramatic. According to a spokesman for Citizen Soldier, a GI rights advocacy group (like a sort of civil liberties union for the military), there are plenty of AWOL American soldiers in Germany, and unless you're a criminal or a traitor (in other words, explained the spokesman, unless you run across the Berlin wall, in uniform, waving a Soviet flag), the army doesn't hunt you down – they don't have the resources or the manpower.

And D'Arby wasn't exactly hiding; he was onstage with the band nearly every night, and during the day he was pressing his tapes on every German record company person he could find. That's how he met KP, Klaus Pieter

Schleinitz, who was working then as a press officer for Ariola International.

KP and D'Arby hit it off immediately. There were many late nights of listening to rock, funk, reggae, and r & b with their good buddy, a German journalist and black music aficionado named Ulli Gueldner. D'Arby, the preacher's son from a strict Pentecostal home, was hearing many of these American pop classics for the first time. If ever there was a college of rock and roll knowledge, D'Arby was in it; saturated with new sounds and new ideas every day, up on stage every night to try things out. The shy, sheltered DeLand teenager was a distant memory.

KP, for his part, realized that this bright, eager black American of a thousand voices who was devouring his record collection was a potential gold mine. He took D'Arby into demo studios in Munich, recorded some tapes, and played them for anyone who'd listen. Roger Trilling, who was then Bill Laswell's manager, remembers hearing a tape of 'KP's guy' in the early eighties when they were looking for singers for Laswell's band, Material. Trilling remembered liking the tape, but nothing ever came of it.

According to various reports, KP either left or got edged out of Ariola, and started up his own label, ON, to which he signed his personal favourites – Kevin Ayers, and the reggae group Chalice. He spent a lot of money – something he was notorious for – but he never

made much. KP, by all accounts, was a lovable hustler and a hard worker, but he had a cult fan's taste in music, and virtually all his projects were commercial disasters; except for one: Terence Trent D'Arby. However, after a successful two years with Touch, everything was now up in the air; Touch was negotiating a record deal, but under the pressure and uncertainty, the band was falling apart.

Then, out of nowhere, KP found a financial backer. A rich fashion wholesaler in Munich had a son who wanted to learn the music business. In return for teaching his son the ropes, the wholesaler offered to fund KP. Suddenly, KP had the means to get his label projects, and D'Arby, rolling. He began spending less time in Germany, and he eventually moved his base of operations to the centre of the game, London.

D'Arby, of course, still had one big problem: the Army. He decided to turn himself in. 'I was starting to like what I was doing too much,' he'd said, 'And I knew if I wanted to go on I had to gamble and take the chance I would go to prison ... so I got myself a real good ol' New York Jewish lawyer ...'

As D'Arby tells it, the army put him on trial and threatened to send him to jail for five years. 'I was being used as an example because there was corruption and bad morale in the unit,' he'd said.

A spokesperson for the US Army wouldn't confirm or deny D'Arby's version of the story, but said that there is no record that soldier Terence Darby was court-martialled. A lesser charge, called an 'administrative reprimand' may have taken place, but the Army does not release such records. (A military lawyer told me that it is very uncommon for the Army to bring court martial proceedings against a soldier simply for a long-term desertion, especially a volunteer recruit.) In any event, D'Arby was officially discharged from the Army on 15 April, 1983.

D'Arby had to go back to the US for his discharge processing, and afterward stayed for a while at home in DeLand. That was when the 'Hendrix hippie' picture had been taken. He'd certainly changed a lot in three years.

There were other, less visible changes, as his former teacher Stan Whitted observed:

'When Terry came home from the Army he came over to my house with a tape of his German band, to ask me what I thought. And whether I thought he should go back to Germany to pursue this music. I listened to the tape and I couldn't believe it was the same person, his singing had matured that much. And I told him to go back there, and try his best . . .

'I think Terry's music was able to develop and mature because he moved away. Any one of those boys I worked with could have become the superstar. With Terry, it was a matter of fate, destiny, being in the right place.

'Look at the amazing, accelerated pace of his success. Could he have done that if he had stayed in the United States? I think not.'

SONOR

TTD

They worked very hard.

KP dogged CBS's London offices, playing his demos for anyone who'd listen. (He had other projects afoot besides D'Arby, long-forgotten bands with names like 'Picnic At the White House'.) Finally, his persistence paid off; a sympathetic A & R person gave him a small amount of 'development deal' money to take D'Arby into a proper studio. KP and D'Arby went in and recorded almost all of the **Introducing the Hardline** LP on that shoestring development budget, less than £35,000.

Meanwhile, Terence Trent D'Arby went to work on the press, chatting up and making friends with rock journalists and industry insiders. A music writer in London remembers D'Arby as being extremely sweet, shy, and obsessively interested in pop lore; he'd call at midnight, and they'd talk shop for hours.

Paolo Hewitt, the staff writer at the **New Musical Express** who wrote the 'New Prince of Pop' cover story, met D'Arby after he saw him perform four songs at the end of a Style Council gig at the Shaw Theatre. 'He already knew me,' Hewitt told me. 'And he knew my writing. He'd been studying the **NME**.

And he'd studied well. Even before his first single came out, Terence Trent D'Arby had the whole British rock press machine behind him. He knew what to say, and how to say it. 'D'Arby seems like something invented by three rock critics on the 'phone,' Charles Shaar Murray observed in **Q**. 'Young, black, American, pretty . . . Highly articulate, enormously well-read and gifted with an awesome knack for self-promotion . . . Perfect.'

When CBS/UK realized that their development-deal singer with the bargain-produced LP was making a stir in the trendiest music circles, they threw a good sized promotion budget behind him. Things happened very quickly; in a matter of weeks, his LP was gold, then platinum. Soon he wasn't just on the cover of music magazines, he was in *every* magazine. Open up **Arena**, or the **Face**, or the **Sunday Times**, and there he was: delicate, fine-boned, with enormous, dreamy eyes, a child-man. Transformation complete.

In that summer of 1987, the Summer of D'Arbymania, he was followed everywhere by photographers eager to catch a snap of him and his latest girlfriend, whoever she was that week. (And there were lots of them: after all, hadn't he told a reporter that he had sex as often as he washed his hair?)

Other managers, and other singers have struggled as hard to break the code of pop stardom. What made this work? Like Stan Whitted, **NME**'s Paolo Hewitt attributed D'Arby's coup to skill, and timing.

'Soul music, black music, has had a real impact in the UK in the last two years. When Terry came along, he fit the musical climate perfectly. He had the voice, and he had the knowledge of pop history. Right from the start, he had the whole press machine behind him. He knows this is a game, and he knows how to play.'

But Hewitt wasn't so sure about D'Arby's ability to repeat his success at home: 'He's learned the Prince lesson well; he refuses to be categorized. But I don't think he'll be big in America, precisely *because* he refuses to categorize himself.'

I spoke to Hewitt in February 1988. By the end of that summer, Terence Trent D'Arby's debut LP had sold over a million copies in the United States.

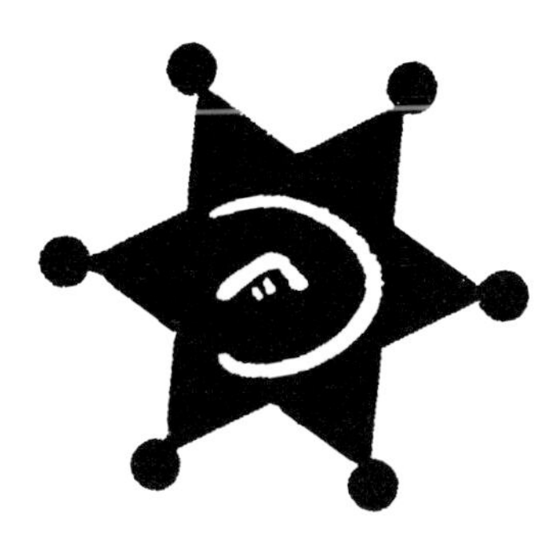

Ha
Ame
chap

rdline:
rica

ter

Hardline: America

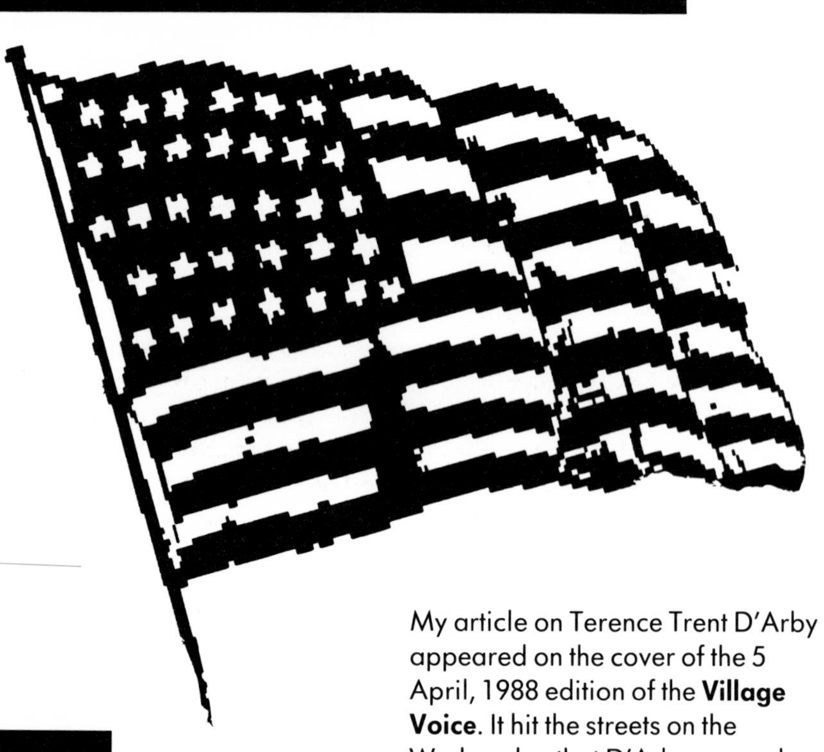

My article on Terence Trent D'Arby appeared on the cover of the 5 April, 1988 edition of the **Village Voice**. It hit the streets on the Wednesday that D'Arby opened a two-show stand at Manhattan's Beacon Theatre, one of the first stops on his 40-city US tour.

The phone started ringing the next day. There wasn't any incendiary or sensational news in the article (especially compared to the racy and suggestive British pieces!): the piece was a textbook investigative report. But Black Rock, nevertheless, was rocking. A colleague at one magazine called me, chuckling, to pass along the news that Marilyn Laverty had informed his editor that I'd 'never work in New York again.'

Later that evening, I got my first call from the British tabloid press. A male correspondent, aggressive and insinuating. He wanted to know where I got the pictures of young Terry Darby. He let me know that if I wanted to pass them to him, there could be 'something in it' for me. He tried to draw me into conversation about the Reverend Darby. Had the Reverend told me his son was about to come back to the church? The hack claimed that right now D'Arby was on the verge of a nervous breakdown – that he had isolated himself in his hotel room and wasn't allowing anyone to see him except Claudine Martinet. 'It's all been too much, too soon, and everybody knows it,' said the tabloid hack.

I asked him how he had

obtained all this information. 'Inside sources,' he told me. I suggested that if he wanted to find out what Reverend Darby thought about his son, he should call and ask the Reverend himself. End of conversation.

Now that they had the **Village Voice** piece to guide them to D'Arby's roots, the UK tabloids descended on DeLand. One of the reporters called Karen Kirkpatrick of the **Sun News** and arranged to buy from her some photographic copies of D'Arby's DeLand yearbook pictures. She made the prints, at her own expense, and sent a package off to England. The tabloid used the pictures; Kirkpatrick is still waiting for her cheque to arrive in the mail.

She continued to cover the latest D'Arby developments. In an excellent **Sun News** article that appeared the following month, in May, she chronicled the reaction to the **Voice** article, and to D'Arby's rising fame in the US. She turned the tables on the hacks, and interviewed them!

And she dug up even more pieces of D'Arby's childhood. The most fascinating of which was a homemade movie made by Terry Darby's junior high school class. She describes his cinematic début: 'He comes strutting through the front door of the old DeLand Junior High with the rest of the kids, slapping a buddy on the shoulder; aware of the hand-held movie camera pointing his way.

'The movie is a treasure of seventies junior high antics . . . It has sound. Here comes a young girl's voice:

"Terry, Terry! How are you?"

"Pretty gooo-ed," the boy replies.

"Are you waiting for the bus, Terry?"

'He steps toward the camera, turns to the side, sticks his chin in the air and says, "No. I'm waiting for a good profile."'

The Reverend and Mrs Darby had not liked my article. Loving parents that they are, they were sensitive to the slightest hint of criticism of their son. They consented to one last interview with Karen Kirkpatrick, and refused to speak to any more reporters.

'We go along as we normally have,' the Reverend said to Kirkpatrick. He told her about the family's trip up to New York (they drove all the way from DeLand) to be close to Terry when he performed at the Grammys in March. The children and Mrs Darby had attended the awards ceremony, he had not. Mrs Darby and her sister had also attended a post-Grammy CBS party. During the visit, Mrs Darby asked her son to write a few words for a time capsule that DeLand Junior High was preparing – it would be placed with other student memorabilia, and uncovered in 2008. Here's what D'Arby wrote:

'I expect (in 20 years) to still be composing, writing, and singing, for it is the task given to me . . . but also directing film, publishing books and eventually conducting my own works for orchestra. And oh, yes, I'll still be famous.'

After D'Arby lost the Grammy for 'Best New Artist' to Jody Watley, he came home to DeLand for a few days with his band. And on Sunday, the whole contingent turned up for services at the Church of Our Lord Jesus Christ.

'He feels that I feel he should go to church when he's in town,' Terence Trent D'Arby's father explained to Karen Kirkpatrick.

D'Arby's New York tour dates were covered by Denis Campbell, an **NME** reporter who had interviewed him previously (Campbell authored the infamous 'I am a genius, point f**king blank' piece). After the first show, Campbell went backstage and asked D'Arby if he'd seen the **Village Voice** cover story, and if he had any comment. Campbell quoted D'Arby as snapping back, 'She just wanted a f**k. I haven't read the story.'

Campbell's **NME** article went on to portray D'Arby as a courageous David, who had his sling well-aimed at the Goliath of CBS's corporate hype machine. He implied that D'Arby was, indeed, fulfilling the mission he'd outlined so many times to UK reporters: challenging the racist, capitalist structures of the US music business. D'Arby was going to become a star on his own terms, just as he'd said he would.

The American rock press had rather different opinions about Terence Trent D'Arby.

The reviews were mixed. 'He needs a new band,' commented Jon Pareles, music critic of **The New York Times**. Pareles thought the Beacon Theatre show was weak, musically speaking: 'His drummer couldn't keep a simple groove.' Jane Scott, rock critic of the Cleveland **Plain Dealer**, found D'Arby's performance 'exciting and powerful', but said that D'Arby needed to let go onstage. He lacked warmth. He was too slick.

Greg Tate, a **Village Voice** colleague who is also a founding member of the Black Rock Coalition (which has nothing to do with CBS, but is an organization of young black rock/funk/pop musicians), really liked D'Arby's **Hardline** début LP. In the 20 October, 1987 issue of the paper, he'd described D'Arby's voice as 'sweet and rough, tough and tender, a many-octave maple syrup poured over sandstone pancakes ... The results may trigger nostalgia, but D'Arby's song is his own.' But after seeing D'Arby live several months later, Tate hedged his praise; 'He's trying ... but it's not quite ... '

Nelson George, a columnist for **Billboard** magazine, is the preeminent writer on black pop in America. He's a well-informed critic's critic, who is the author of a bestselling biography of Michael Jackson, and, more recently, the definitive history of Motown Records. During the wave of American coverage of D'Arby's album, Grammy appearance, and tour, I waited to see what Nelson George would write, thinking that he would have the most interesting take on the return of the DeLand native. But his byline never appeared on a D'Arby piece. So, I called him to see if he had an opinion on the man and his music. As it turned out, he had quite a bit to say.

(Nelson George) I have several thoughts about D'Arby, and they go in this order: When I first heard about him, I was in England, I guess six months to a year before his record came out here. I was in London at a party. I was asking all sorts of people what's hot, what's happening here, and everybody mentioned D'Arby. People mentioned other groups, but almost uniformly they mentioned D'Arby. They all said that he was the new thing, that he was a combination of James Brown and Jackie Wilson. Not just people from CBS, but everybody in general said that this was the exciting new act over there. So that piqued my interest. Then I read a couple of interviews that he did, particularly the one with Charles Shaar Murray. Which really intrigued me, because he seemed very political, very smart, and obviously a little cocky, but that cockiness together with his apparent political insights made for an exciting mix. I thought, well this is interesting. If this guy is half as good at performing as he is with his brain, this guy could be something really special.

That's what I thought initially. Then I heard the record. 'If You Let Me Stay' was a good record but ... it didn't really state anything, like it was supposed to be a statement record, but it didn't really say anything. He seemed to be doing what Paul Young did, but not as well. But I thought there was something there. On the album overall there were some brilliant things. Like that one done acapella, 'Untitled' – the sort of tone poem? That was really brilliant. 'Sign Your Name' was excellent. 'Wishing Well', when I heard that I knew it would be a black radio hit when they put it out here, I was surprised that wasn't the first single, 'cause I knew black radio wouldn't play 'If You Let Me Stay'. I certainly didn't think the album, overall, owned up to D'Arby's hype about it, but it was a promising record. Showed this guy had a lot of talent, definitely had some thoughts in his head. But I saw real room for growth.

And then the hype took off in America, and I heard a lot about him. The hype thing said he was the greatest thing since Jackie

Wilson – now this was mostly coming from people who'd never seen Jackie Wilson perform! Or for that matter, who had never seen James Brown in his prime, like I had, like people I knew had. The hype really put me on edge a bit.

I happened to run into him on the street during this time, on 6th Avenue. He and a little blond Englishwoman. I was going towards the CBS building, and he was coming out of it. And he's, you know he's a very distinctive looking character. Well, I went up and said, 'Aren't you Terence Trent D'Arby?' And he said, 'Yes I am.' He was very shy, apparently he knew my face, knew my name from Billboard. He was very friendly, and we just chatted for a few minutes. It was interesting to run into him like that. This was well before the record came out.

Anyway, I finally saw him at the Ritz, the first time he came over here. He had done the Roxy in LA just before. And I really, really didn't like him. I thought he was corny, to be quite honest. What he looked like to me was . . . well, to begin with, he was dressed like Mick Jagger on the TAMI show. He had the same kind of shoes, the same kind of outfit. Was it intentional? Who knows. He's very self-conscious about that kind of stuff. D'Arby reminded me of Mick Jagger imitating James Brown. There's that famous scene in the TAMI show, where James Brown comes on and the next sequence is the Rolling Stones. And then you see Jagger sort of doing his version of James Brown. That's what Terence looked like to me. Once-removed. His influences didn't seem to be the actual r & b people that people were comparing him to. He looked as if he was influenced by the people who were influenced by the people. And I thought his band kind of sucked. They didn't really kick. The background singers were weak. I was really disappointed, and I got kind of bored midway through. The set wasn't very well-paced. It didn't hit me. Paul Young was sitting behind me and he left early too. I didn't get it. I didn't think he was nearly as interesting live as the record.

But I wasn't going to hold it against him. It was his first gig in New York, and the guy's bound to be uptight, right? What made me begin to be much more sceptical about D'Arby was the first few interviews he did over here. And the fact that he didn't do any interviews. He seemed to me to be – and maybe this is part of the marketing of him, I really don't know what machinations went on – but it seemed as if he was backing away from the political talk that had marked his statements in London. And I thought that was part of a conscious strategy, not to make him political by keeping him away from the press. When he did talk, he didn't talk about the United States' government policies, as he had in England. Or about why he left the US. In America he was being marketed as a teenybopper idol, which was a great departure from the way he had been positioned in the UK. And I began to think that maybe the whole thing was a pose. With him being so conscious of how the critics work, and how the media works, he may

have realized that, being a black American in England, the political, antagonistic posture was the right one to take over there. To talk bad about America would sell. And here in America, to be the more reclusive, Prince-like figure was a better strategy. So I began to see D'Arby's whole thing as sort of a con.

I wanted to interview him at one point. I was really curious to ask him about all this. That was the time he was over here and he 'wasn't doing any interviews'. I did run into him one time at the restaurant called Jezebels. He was in there, they had had him talking to a bunch of black radio people because CBS was trying to get him on black radio. This is before 'Sign Your Name' and 'Wishing Well'. He struck me as being a very nice guy. I hear a lot of bad things about him, mostly from women, who say he was surly. But he was never surly in my presence.

Then I saw him at the Grammy awards. And I just thought that he was trying so damn hard to be important. He started off well, and then he went over the line. It just seemed like he went on too long. He was trying to make a point: I'm an important motherfucker. I'm a major, major talent, I'm a star. You people should be paying attention to me. I'm the next shit. Which is a perfectly legitimate thing. He was trying to do Michael Jackson on Motown. That kind of statement. And following Michael Jackson. That just shows the guy has balls. I don't have any problem with that. I don't think he succeeded. But I respect D'Arby's aspirations. I only question, at this point, how much of him has to do with a vision that has an integrity, and how much is just a more sophisticated media-conscious strategy.

I still think he has the potential to be a major artist. I don't think he's a major artist now, despite the fact that he thinks so. Maybe his record company wants you to think so. I believe he needs to work on his singing. He's got a good instrument, he can sing better, and I think if he continues singing the way he sings live, he's gonna really fuck up his voice, just technically. He's singing in his throat a lot, very raw and aggressively. A lot of young untrained singers do the same thing. That stuff'll give you nodes like crazy.

I thought the record showed more maturity and more successful ambition than his show does. He performs like he has a chip on his shoulder. But I don't get the feeling that chip has been earned. I don't get the impression that his life has been that rough, you know what I mean? And he's trying to compete on that level. I just feel artifice. That's my reaction. I look at the hype he's gotten in America, then I look at Al B Sure, Keith Sweat, Bobby Brown . . . I think that all those kids could all kick D'Arby's ass on stage. Even though Al doesn't sing as well as he does. To me, D'Arby was not the most exciting young black artist of the year, not by a long shot.

What do you think would've happened if D'Arby had brought his demo tape around to Black A & R departments in New York instead of in London?

I think a couple of the tunes would've made it through. 'Wishing Well' and 'Sign Your Name'. I don't think any Black A & R department would've picked in 1988 for 'If You Let Me Stay' to be the single. I don't think it would've even got on the record. He's trying to do something interesting, obviously, which is to mix a sort of rock sensibility with an r & b soul thing. Which didn't used to be a radical mix, but it is today. Being from England helps all artists over here, white or black. It especially helps black artists. Being from England is a real plus at this point. If he'd come up from Florida with that tape, he would've had a harder time.

I don't think he has a black audience. I think he has some black fans, some black folks who bought his album. But I don't think he has a real base, loyal audience among blacks here, not yet. I think he could have one with his next album. I think of the young, the 'new jack' generation, between Al B Sure, Keith Sweat, New Edition, any major rap artist, and you ask the average black teenager, 'Where does D'Arby fit?' and they would tell you someplace way below there. Unless you're talking to a black kid growing up in a very white environment, very influenced by the MTV thing. At this point D'Arby doesn't have a hardcore black audience. He has some blacks who are interested in him. It'll take another record for him to

have that. I perceive his audience in America to be white teenage girls. Which is kind of disappointing in terms of what I thought he was, or trying to be. He wants to seem dangerous, but he doesn't seem dangerous. He just seems kind of quirky.

Boy George and Sade . . . I think they were the models for what CBS did with D'Arby. Both of those artists had tremendous success in England, and also over here on black radio. I think CBS saw D'Arby as a very visual, MTV artist with a Prince-like crossover potential that they could take to black and white radio. And because he was from England, and very exotic-looking, they could get the kind of visual exposure for him that an ordinary black artist in America can't get.

Whether they told D'Arby to keep his mouth shut over here, or whether he decided to himself that it was prudent to keep his mouth shut, it really doesn't matter. He kept his mouth shut. The effect was that there was a vacuum of information that was filled by the CBS hype and by the videos, etcetera.

I asked George if he'd read the true story of D'Arby's adolesence; about how he'd been a shy, self-conscious teenager.

(George, *laughing*) He's very self conscious. He's still skinny and a little wimpy. I don't think that's changed. I mean, him and the motorcycle in the video is a little ridiculous. I said, come on. You know what I mean? What are you doin', man. He's the kind of guy you want to sit down and say, 'Look, brother, what the fuck is up with this motorcycle shit? This shit is not working, give it up!'

But the thing he did over here was off-putting. I mean, I know women who went up to him who were big fans of his . . . he was pretty nasty to a lot of people over here, especially women. One woman at Billboard who was a big big fan of his, had his picture up in her office, she went up to him at a party, said 'I really love your work', and he wouldn't even acknowledge her. Just stared right through her.

What do you think D'Arby has to do to really break through as the major star he wants to be in the US?

Well, I don't think he has to do a lot of interviews, but he has to do some interviews. It seems like he wants to be this very elusive character, but I think he needs to go and visit radio stations, and do

in-stores. I think it would help him a lot if he got more of a feeling for the people who like him, more personal contact. I think he should be doing this kind of stuff now, actually, before the next record comes out, before be begins recording it. I'd like to see him be open to some other influences musically. England right now is full of some very great retro r & b songwriters, white and black. I think it'd be good for him to collaborate with another melody writer. There's a certain sameness to his songs, and that would help the music. He and Mick Hucknall together would be interesting. Lamont Dozier is over there, he does a lot of good stuff. Robin Miller who does the Sade stuff. Some of the people who work over at Jive records. He seems to be so much into his own head, working with other people could open him up. He seems to want to be Prince, but not everybody can be Prince. Like Prince he wants to control everything, and I don't think that's possible. I think it would help a lot if he had a better stage show. A better band. For the kind of stuff he wants to do, especially when you get into the James Brown thing, you need to have people who can really groove. Musicians who know how to fall into it and it just kicks! and stays there. His band could never do that.

He needs to make better music, and take the chip off his shoulder. I think if he talked a little more about his feelings about . . . I think there's a mood in this country, and . . . it depends on what he wants to be, but . . . if he wants to be a political/social figure, he's gonna have to be a little more explicit about what he believes in. I think there's a lot of confusion over what he believes in.

He doesn't write songs about what the interviews were about. Except for the 'Untitled' thing, which obliquely deals with some things. For someone who's as well-read as he is . . . he knows better. And if he wants to be considered a political/social figure, he's going to have to write a '1999'. Like a Prince, or a Marvin Gaye, or like the other people he considers his idols. All of whose best work deals with various issues. The Hardline . . . there was nothing hard about that. What Hardline? The whole package suggested a political stance, and it didn't deliver. It's the whole posing thing: politics is just another suit of clothes to wear when he needs to.

I thought about writing about him a number of times. But I really wasn't sure what position to take in the sense that he was doing well, but clearly he wasn't a significant artist for the audience I write about, and for. There were so many more interesting things going on.

Take someone like Sade, who started out with a similar kind of hype, to some degree, her look, coming from England, etcetera. And she's become a very familiar part of the black music scene in America, very respected for what she does.

George compared D'Arby to another black singer of the same generation now coming up in the US charts, named Bobby Brown.

There was a lot of rumours about Brown, people were saying he was a drug addict and things. A lot of bad stuff came out about the kid. Well, he made a record which was like a rap record, except he was singing, about what people thought about him, and in the songs made it clear that he really didn't give a fuck about what people thought. Now if Terence Trent D'Arby took his political intelligence, and made records like that, about his experience as a black person in England, and living in Germany, and being in the Army . . . then he'd be winning, and he'd win big. That would be a statement. It would be unique as well. I mean, that's the guy I thought that he was, from the interviews. But that wasn't what was on the record.

I think of a Terence Trent D'Arby, and all the hype surrounding him, and say, 'Come on! There's people who really *do* this thing.'

Maybe the American critics didn't buy the D'Arby myth, but that didn't stop the public from buying D'Arby's record. His début album, **The Hardline According to Terence Trent D'Arby**, sold well over a million copies, sat in the Top 30 charts for most of 1988, and spun off two Top Ten singles, 'Wishing Well', and 'Sign Your Name'.

'The press doesn't have a tenth of the influence here that it does in the UK,' **New York Times** pop critic Jon Pareles pointed out during a conversation about D'Arby. In the US, the key avenues for promoting a new act are television and radio. D'Arby had the Today Show, MTV, Entertainment Tonight, and the full marketing power of CBS Records on his side. He didn't need the press. On this side of the Atlantic, It's much better to let the music – and the money – do the talking, and via the airwaves, not print.

But even in America, money only goes so far. And the most amazing sales figures aren't sufficient to propel a singer into the élite pantheon of pop stardom. D'Arby is a success, but he still isn't a 'major artist'. Despite his record company's efforts, people aren't paying attention to him the way they did to the young Springsteen, or to Prince. He still lacks something that can't be learned by rote. Call it what you will: mystique; presence; the ability to push an audience beyond its limits, and help them, as Jim Morrison wrote, to 'break on through to the other side'. In his first year in America, D'Arby sold plenty of records, but he didn't catch fire.

The artist who *did*, and went on to become the pop event of 1988, was a young black singer who, ironically enough, also breaks the music-biz stereotypes. Tracy Chapman's stark, unadorned folk songs place her well outside the r & b category, and certainly far away from the world of Top-40 pop. Her personal style is unconventional: no makeup, no posturing, androgynous, decidedly unglamorous; and she turned the record industry on its head. Her début album soared to Number One, as did her single, 'Fast Car'. When she performed that song, alone with her guitar, for the gathered top brass of the American record industry at the 1989 Grammy awards ceremony in February, she was received in an awed, respectful silence. (Quite a different reception from the one that D'Arby had received only the year before on the nationally-televised awards show.) Every time Chapman walked on stage to collect an award, she was greeted with roaring cheers. She went home with nearly every major prize in her pocket.

Terence Trent D'Arby won his first Grammy that same night, for best album in the r & b male vocal category. But it must have been a rather disappointing consolation prize for a singer who considers himself part of the pop, not the r & b market. On the one hand, part of him must have been glad to see another 'rebel' getting through; but another part must have been very frustrated: Chapman was receiving the accolades and acceptance that he himself was still struggling for.

D'Arby didn't collect his Grammy in person. At the time he was back home in his new house in Drayton Park, Islington, writing songs and laying tracks for his second album. He was busy with something else, too. On 31 December, 1988, his steady girlfriend, makeup artist Mary Vango, gave birth to their first child, a 4lb 11oz daughter named Seraphina. Born prematurely, but doing fine.

The proud father was keeping a low profile. Shortly after his American tour, he fired his gregarious manager KP, and replaced him with protective, efficient Claudine Martinet. After returning to London in the summer of 1988, he practically turned into the invisible man, in comparison with the wild, publicity-ridden summer of 1987. He was reputedly hard at work on his music.

Second albums are crucial in the development of a pop career. For D'Arby, this is especially true. As Nelson George indicated, a lot of US critics agree that D'Arby has potential, but they're waiting to see what he comes up with next. If he merely does **Hardline, Part II**, they'll eat him for breakfast. He has to expand, take chances, show that he's maturing. Then he's in with a chance of a long, prestigious career.

Can he do it? It's impossible to predict. But, based on the discoveries about his adolescence and early career, it seems so. At the very least, he will spend every ounce of energy he has trying to prove that he deserves a place in the rock and roll hall of fame. And the skinny boy who made himself into a boxing champ stands a good chance of succeeding at this challenge, too.

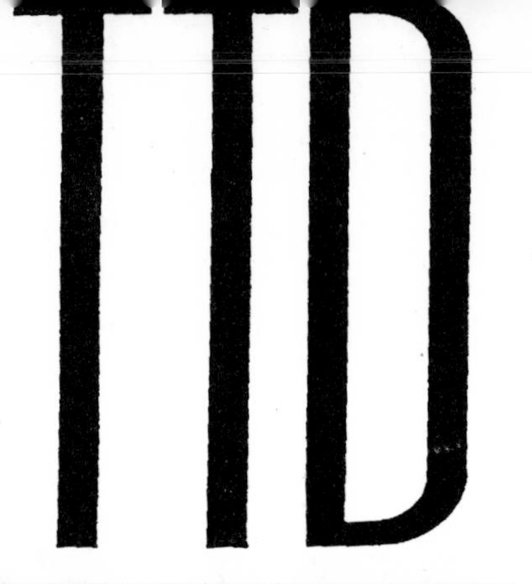

D'Arby has been motivated in his life so far by two forces: his frustration, and his ambition. It's obvious, from his parents' and others' recollections, that he was a precocious, intelligent and sensitive boy. It's also clear that he didn't get the kind of recognition for his talents that he craved. Other boys were better singers, other students got better grades. His home town was too small and provincial to appreciate his unique qualities. This frustrated and angered him, and those bitter feelings have endured to this day. His need to be noticed has driven him ever since. It is a powerful need that has been the fuel for three complete and remarkable self-transformations.

'He's such a chameleon,' Karen Kirkpatrick exclaimed during one of our long discussions about D'Arby. 'But underneath all the masks, he's still a child begging for attention.' The shy DeLand preacher's son, whom his classmates thought 'kinda goofy', turned himself into a well-developed boxer. When that role got him out of his home town, and out of the US, he achieved another transformation, becoming the cool, hip rebel of the Germany years. In London, he re-created himself as the thin, boyish soul man of the moment.

Each transformation worked brilliantly. And today Terry Darby has become Terence Trent D'Arby: man, father, successful musician. There's only one mountain left to climb, and he is quietly climbing it even now. All his hopes and fears, passions and ambitions are tied up in his quest for critical acceptance. Only now he's not reaching for the approval of DeLand, he's reaching for the world.

And that's a tough one. D'Arby's ability to mould and re-make himself in the images of his heroes is considerable, but if you want to be a hero, you have to have your own image, not a pastiche of other people's. You have to have something to say, something that no one else says in quite the same way. If the reaction of the US critics is any indication, D'Arby hasn't accomplished this. Not yet.

But it's possible that he'll be able to achieve that final self-transformation, and find his own face, and his own voice. Terence Trent D'arby has some powerful passions and energies locked up inside him. If he has the will, and the courage, to let these emotions come out in his music, without filtering them through the masks and images of his heroes, he's going to have an amazing second album.

There is, of course, another possibility. There is a road that has been open to him since childhood. It's a road that stretches out in the opposite direction to the one he's been following since he left DeLand to join the Army and see the world. But the D'Arby family believes it's a road that all other roads eventually join, including that of a rock and roll star. Terence Trent D'Arby has changed directions and faces many time in his short life. so it wouldn't be at all surprising if he woke up one morning, phoned his manager, his agent, his record company, and the entire editorial staff of the **New Musical Express** to tell them one last bit of controversial, headline-grabbing news: forget the concert tours. Turn off the press machine. My father was right.